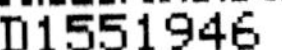

THE INCAS

HISTORY AND TREASURES OF AN ANCIENT CIVILIZATION

WHITE STAR PUBLISHERS

CONTENTS

TEXT
CAROLINA ORSINI

EDITORIAL DIRECTION
VALERIA MANFERTO DE FABIANIS

COLLABORATING EDITORS
LAURA ACCOMAZZO
GIORGIO FERRERO

GRAPHIC DESIGN
PAOLA PIACCO

WS White Star Publishers® is a registered trademark property of Edizioni White Star s.r.l.

© 2008, 2012 White Star s.r.l.
Piazzale Luigi Cadorna, 6
20123 Milan, Italy
www.whitestar.it

Revised edition

Translation text: Davide Arnold Lamagni
Translation captions: Glenn Debattista

ISBN 978-88-544-0711-4
2 3 4 5 6 24 23 22 21 20

Printed in China

1 - This rod finial, made of copper and silver (height 3.5 inches/9 cm) and shaped like a bird, is from the Peruvian coast and dates to the period of Incan domination (Dumbarton Oaks Collection, Washington, D.C.).

2-3 - The city of Machu Picchu was built on the orders of Inca Pachacutec in the 15th century.

4-5 - The mural decorates an important Moche ceremonial center: Huaca de la Luna (The Temple of the Moon), near Trujillo.

6 - Among the Moche the earring was a symbol of rank, worn by the elite (Gold Museum, Lima).

INTRODUCTION

Upon their arrival in Peru in 1532 the Spanish found a highly organized kingdom extending over a good 775,000 sq. miles (2 million sq km). The peoples governing it called it Tawantinsuyu ("The Four Parts Together"). The Incas, Children of the Sun, as they defined themselves, managed the amazing feat of organizing the most hostile of territories in less than 90 years.

It is not by chance, therefore, that in the course of the following centuries Europeans associated the Inca people with a legendary and unique history which overshadowed preceding peoples to which the Inca are indebted to an extent which is hard to ignore.

The millenary Andean tradition which the Inca learnt from, in fact, began a few years before the birth of Christ, when on the Peruvian coast there were monumental settlements associated with enormous ceremonial centers which based their survival on a complex domination of the territory and a highly developed agricultural technology. But it is especially from the tradition that developed in the 1st millennium AD that Inca culture really developed. This took place in the southern-central Andes, with the Tiwanaku culture (in the Lake Titicaca area in Bolivia) with the Huari culture (in the area where the city of Ayacucho now stands). This was the cultural basis that fueled the Inca civilization, among others. Some cardinal elements, which allowed the development of the Inca Empire, such as the road and numbering systems, were already well developed during the Huari era. The Huari asserted themselves as the main power in the whole Andean area. They did this by exporting a social and economical model in the Cuzco area. This model can be most easily seen in the chessboard structure of cities, the most evident example in the Inca area being the imposing site of Pikillacta. By elaborating the previous tradition with an original synthesis, the Inca managed to surpass the Huari model in terms of size and power, achieving the most extensive dominion of the Andean area. We will never know whether the Empire of the "Four Parts Together" would have lasted over time: attracted by the news of a land full of riches, the area became the conquering ground of a group of Spanish adventurers captained by Francisco Pizarro.

In the minds of the *conquistadores*, the Inca were the custodians of an exorbitant richness – leading to the legend of Paititi, the city of gold much sought after by European adventurers, and the land of utopian democracy dear to the Enlightenment thinkers of the 18th century. The power of the empire, the albeit precarious balance achieved to govern such a vast territory and the complex Andean thought which materialized in a multi-faceted society like that of the Incas contributed to feed the European image of a sought-after exotic empire to be used but also admired. In the last ten years Peruvian politicians have used the empire of the "Four Parts Together" to evoke an image of power and economic rebirth for the nation, knowing they could play on a very suggestive metaphor.

Even though today one cannot avoid associating the Inca dominion over the Andean area with the great powers of the Old Continent, a more capillary knowledge of local archaeology has led to a review of the paradigms associated with the fame of the Children of the Sun. A melting pot of different

8 - This Sicán-Lambayeque style stone and gold mosaic pendent comes from the north coast of Peru. It depicts an almond-eyed figure with a prominent nose (Gold Museum, Lima).

9 - This cat-shaped painted wood vase (or *quero*) dates back to the first colonial era (1680-1720) and comes from Cuzco. *Queros* were used during ceremonial occasions (Museo de América, Madrid).

ethnic groups and languages, the land of "The Four Parts Together" was never an empire in the Western sense of the term. In fact, it was not a dominion with precise boundaries, but rather a network of alliances and reciprocal agreements that the Incas had built and maintained until the arrival of the Spanish. Heirs to a millenary tradition of intelligent use of resources, technology and a refined social organization system, the Incas conducted a rapid and aggressive expansion. This allowed them to prevail and impose a system of vassalage on many peoples, not only in the Cuzco Valley, where the first conflicts took place. This dominion extended well beyond the original boundaries of contemporary Peru, reaching into Ecuador, Argentina and Chile. The ductility of the Andean social organization allowed the Incas to set up a similar taxation system for different peoples, however separated by ethnicity or language and traditions.

In construction art and technology the Incas distinguished themselves through their clearly recognizable language, characterized by an abstract symbolism which adapted well to an "international style." Some aspects of the social organization, the rapport with the territory, and the indigenous religiosity – cultural manifestations which the Spanish tried to fight for the whole colonial period – still survive today, transformed and enriched by new elements in the current Andean cultures, especially in the Cuzco Valley area.

This book will attempt to explain how the Tawantinsuyu formed their state in such a short time, and it will try to recount the intricate story of the mythical origins of these people. The Incas never used an alphabet-based form of writing: most of their known history derives from the observations and narratives of the Spanish when they came into contact with them, and from what was recorded in native and mestizo chronicles during the colonial period. The fragmentary and often contradictory nature of the story must be accepted; it is based on incomplete if not biased information which must be weighed against evidence from archaeological remains.

It seems incredible that many aspects of what was the most extensive dominion of the American continent are still so hazy. Archaeology in the Peruvian Andes still has a long way to go. What can be read in the chronicles can tell us only a small part of the story of the multi-faceted Inca society. Furthermore, while some chroniclers have provided us with very acute observations, almost ethnographical, regarding the customs and costumes of these people, others were not capable of this or were unwilling to understand the Inca world. This is why many fundamental aspects of the life of the Children of the Sun are still being debated. These include the exact sequence of their rulers, the true extent of the empire, and the chronology of the occupation of the Cuzco Valley. Thus it is very difficult to pinpoint the exact beginning of the Inca civilization.

One of the fathers of Andean archaeology, the American researcher John Rowe, established a "master sequence" of Andean cultures, starting from the observation of local changes which took place in the Ica Valley, a small valley on the coast south of Lima. Since then, sixty years have gone by and researchers have continued to use this master sequence, establishing how the beginning of the so-called Third Horizon, or Inca period, coincides with the Inca conquest of the Ica area. That is apparently when the "imperial" (an inappropriate word for the Andean area) phase of Tawantinsuyu history began. The previous period, which corresponds to the first steps of the Inca people to assert themselves in the Cuzco Valley, seems to belong to a phase of the Andean history in which there was no unifying or super-regional culture, but in which a series of small groups lived side by side, interacting at a local level. This earlier phase is only known through written accounts of different legends, with a varying degree of historical basis. Our narration will begin from here, from this same "mythical time."

11 - This gold-plated ornament (height 5.1 inches/13 cm) depicts two figures, perhaps shamans, wearing a crescent-shaped headdress, in a trance. It comes probably from the Santuario Histórico del Bosque de Pomac region. It reflects the Sicán-Lambayeque culture, and dates to the 11th-13th centuries (Bruning

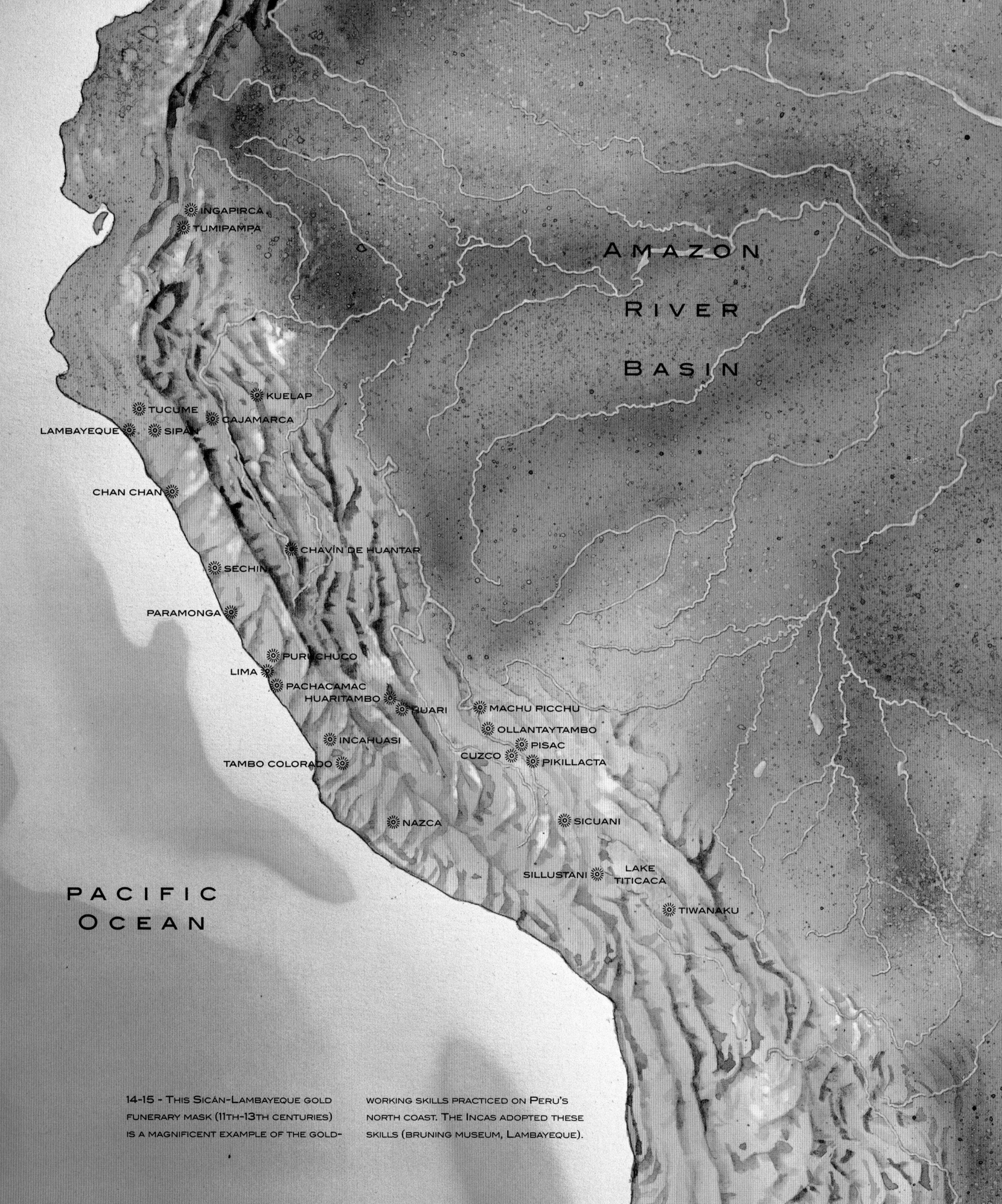

14-15 - This Sicán-Lambayeque gold funerary mask (11th-13th centuries) is a magnificent example of the gold-working skills practiced on Peru's north coast. The Incas adopted these skills (Bruning Museum, Lambayeque).

PRE-INCA CULTURES AND THE QOTAKALLI PERIOD
(1000 BC - AD 600)

Various traditions established themselves during the so-called Ancient Horizon (1000-200 BC) in different areas of the Peruvian territory. Pre-eminent among these was the Chavín culture (named after the ceremonial center in the northern central Sierra). During the so-called Ancient Intermediate Period (0-800 AD), the Moche, Nazcan and Recuay cultures developed and expanded. The first half of the 1st millennium AD was a time of fervor throughout the Peruvian territory. In the Cuzco area, a density of settlements began to be seen in the southwestern reaches of the Huatanay River. Here, we find a type of ceramics known as *Qotakalli*. Evidence of exotic-type ceramics led to the supposition that even though the lesser lords of Cuzco Valley had never moved beyond their borders, they had inter-regional trade relations – especially with the southern high plateau on the banks of the shores of Lake Titicaca.

THE HUARI IN THE CUZCO VALLEY
(AD 600-1000)

Around AD 500, an aggressive people came from the central southern area of the Andes – from the Ayacucho *sierra* north of Cuzco – to expand their influence in some important points of what is today, Peru. The Huari were the first power to move beyond the borders of their own ethnic territory. They built the majestic city of Pikillacta, in the Cuzco area, to exploit the local agricultural potential. The cohabitation with the ethnic groups in the area – which had lived there since the *Qotakalli* period – may have become critical. In any case, the location was abandoned and burned. The ephemeral presence of the Huari was an important stage in the development of the Huatanay Valley region. In fact, some innovations, brought there by the Huari, were absorbed as already acquired elements in successive stages in the area and were included in the "cultural heritage" of the Incas.

THE KILLKE PERIOD AND THE FIRST INCAS
(AD 1000-1400)

After the Huari's loss of power, the regional expansion phase began again in the Cuzco area and a style of ceramics which became known as *Killke* was widespread. This type of ceramic ware has been found in a vast area of the Huatanay Valley and even in the foundations of the most ancient buildings of Cuzco, the city which was to become the capital of the future Inca empire. This phase saw great activity in the construction of sites and farming terraces and in the occupation of new territories. This era also probably marked the settlements of the first Inca sovereigns, whose names are passed down to us by the chronicles: Manco Capac (a legendary figure and the first founder of the dynasty), Sinchi Roca, Lloque Yupanqui and Mayta Capac. The Incas, from a small ethnic group that had cohabited with other groups of people, began to acquire a certain degree of power on the regional level with the reign of the sixth Inca, the Inca Roca. Viracocha, the eighth Inca, began an expansionist policy toward the territories to the southeast, where he succeeded in prevailing over various groups (the Cana and the Canchi).

THE EXPANSION OF THE EMPIRE
(AD 1440-1493)

In the 1440s, Pachacutec Inca Yupanqui ascended the throne. Under this sovereign, the Incas began to enact an aggressive expansionistic policy and to carry out lengthy military campaigns: in the southern sierra to conquer the Titicaca area; to the north to gain the fertile region of Cajamarca, and on the northern coast, where they subjugated the Chimú kingdom. The southern coast was also annexed both through military campaigns and alliances with local lords. Pachacutec inaugurated the custom of the reigning Inca appointing the successor to the throne, and he nominated his son, Topa Yupanqui, who was to continue with his expansionist policy and to become a skillful military leader.

THE CONSOLIDATION OF THE EMPIRE
(AD 1493-1528)

After the death of Topa Yupanqui, in 1493, the son of Huayna Capac ascended the throne. He focused on consolidating the conquests made in the past and even subjugated the Chachapoyas' so-called "Kingdom of the Clouds," in the Marañon area. He exerted much energy to conquer Ecuador, where he established the administrative center of Tumipampa, a sort of northern capital, where he settled until his death in about 1528.

THE STRUGGLE FOR THE THRONE
(AD 1528-1532)

The death of Huayna Capac occurred at the same time as the death of his son Ninan Cuyuchi, whom he had appointed to be his successor. As a result, Huayna Capac 's other two sons – Atahuallpa and Huascar – fought each other for the throne. This rivalry soon led to a fierce civil war that caused numerous deaths among the population before Huascar was captured. In his triumphal march to Cuzco, Atahuallpa encountered a group of foreigners who asked him for audience: the Spanish, led by Francisco Pizarro.

THE CONQUEST AND THE NEO-INCA STATE
(AD 1532-1572)

The encounter took place in Cajamarca in 1532: Athuallpa was taken prisoner and obliged to collect a ransom in gold to save his life. He was nonetheless sentenced to death, and executed only a few months later. The Spanish crowned Manco Inca, who after a short time was able to escape from the Spanish interference and to organize a not successful attempt to regain the territories. Manco Inca retreated to the area of Vilcabamba, where he founded an independent Neo-Inca state which, upon his death, was maintained untill Tupac Amaru, the last Inca ruler, was captured and put to death in 1572.

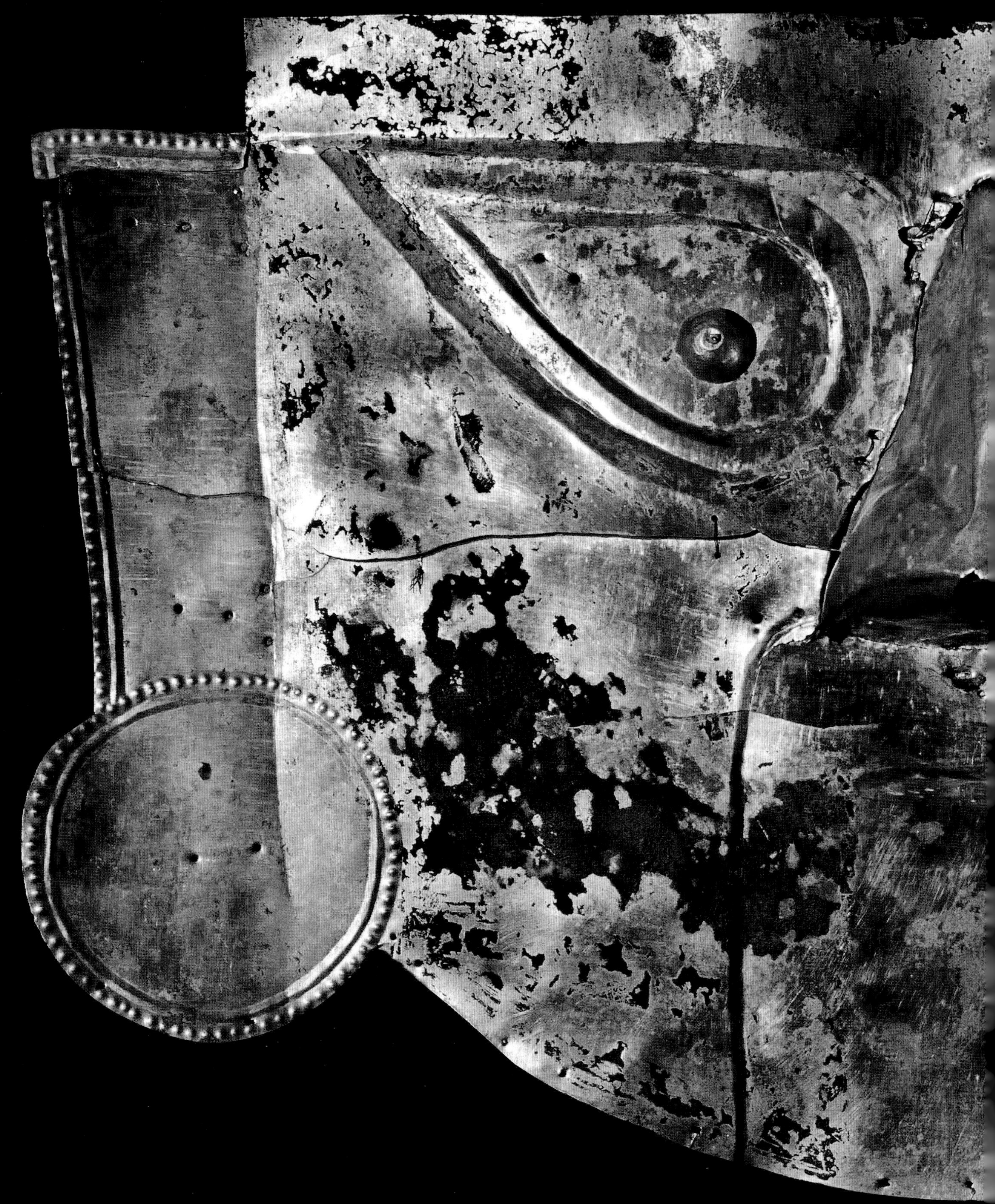

1

PRE-INCA SOCIETIES IN THE CUZCO VALLEY

THE ENVIRONMENT

The Inca civilization is the final expression of a long transformation process involving Andean societies. This explains the formation of an empire, which as we will see, grew to its maximum size in fewer than 90 years. To understand this process, it will be necessary to review briefly some of the milestones preceding the incredible Inca parable. We will pay particular attention to the history of the valley of the Huatanay River, a fertile portion of the Southern Andes, rich in water sources which flow from the many mountain heights, covered in snow all year round (at altitudes of over 13,000 ft/4000 m). This area was very good for economic development and soon witnessed the consolidation of the Inca settlement. In a few years it became a metropolis – Cuzco – with more than 20,000 inhabitants: the physical and symbolic center of the Inca empire.

In Peru there are three adjacent ecological areas that run parallel to the Pacific Ocean: a coastal area, a mountain area, and the Amazon area. The coastal area, or *Chala*, is essentially desert: imposing channels built in the first millennia BC allowed the land to be used for agricultural purposes. Peru's coastal populations could in any case count on the edible resources of one of the world's richest oceans; this explains why today the *Chala* is one of the most populated areas in the whole country.

The coastal climate is strongly influenced by the Humboldt Current (named after the famous German geographer and naturalist). This cold current causes marine temperatures to sink to arctic levels. Thus we have a sea at a tropical latitude with a curious fauna of seals, sea lions, and even a particular species of penguin (the Humboldt penguin). Proceeding eastward the ground starts to rise, with moderate inclinations (the so-called *yungas* between 1500 and 7500 ft (450 and 2300 m) above sea level) where fruit and sugar cane are grown. In the central part of the country we have the Andes range (from 7,500 to 21,300 ft/450 to 6500 m above sea level). This was the most populated area in the Inca period and had the highest agricultural capacity. In fact, in the lower parts of the val-

leys on the eastern and western sides, there is the ecological area called *Quechua* (from 7,500 to 11,500 ft/450 to 3500 m), which has a moderate climate (with abundant seasonal precipitation, concentrated between December and May). This is good for cereal and fruit cultivation (it was not by chance that Cuzco, the general headquarters of the Inca empire, arose in the Quechua area of the southern part of the Andean range).

Even the most impervious areas of the Andean range were used for pasture. These have plateaus at between 12,500 and 16,000 ft/3650 and 4875 m, the altitude above which there is perennial snow. Nowadays the high plateaus are essentially used for cattle of European origin, whilst in the pre-Hispanic period they were grazing land for camelidae such as llamas and alpacas. They were also used for the cultivation of a kind of tuber particularly resistant to the cold. There are thousands of Peruvian autochthonous species of tubers and these formed the basis of the local diet, both before the Spanish and to this day.

The third area, moving from west to east, is the Amazon area (from the so-called *Ceja de selva*, at around 6500 ft/2000 m to the Amazon forest at sea level). The gradual slopes are covered in thick vegetation and orchids. This is the most typical image of Peru, as Machu Picchu, the renowned archaeological site, is in the *Ceja de selva* area northwest of Cuzco. This area was populated and used not only for its agricultural potential and the resources of the river and forest, but also because the habitat was ideal for the cultivation the most important medicinal and sacred plant of Andean area, i.e., coca *(Erythroxylum coca)*. This plant has been used for relief from hunger and tiredness, as an instrument of divination, and as a funerary offer from ancient times to today.

In the forest area true small-scale agriculture was practiced and the abundant local fauna was much exploited. In particular, birds with colorful plumes and felines were used, and prestigious ornaments were made from feathers and pelts. These were traded by the locals with the Andean and coastal peoples.

17 - One of the most typical expressions of Moche artistic representation was stirrup-style portrait vases (Maahun, Trujillo).

18 left - On his back this male figure carries an *arybalo*, a typical Inca container used to transport and store liquids (Ethnologisches Museum, Berlin).

18 right - This famous Moche terracotta jug (8th century AD) portrays a sacrificial scene taking place on a mountain top (Ethnologisches Museum, Berlin).

19 left - This headdress, of the Chimú or Chancay culture (11th -14th centuries) is built upon a stiff framework (wood) covered with a feather mosaic and finished with gold decorations. It was matched with a pair of earrings made using the same technique (Gold Museum, Lima).

19 right - This Chimú two-colored feather crown, 6.2 inches (16 cm) in height, dates to the 11th-14th centuries. It is decorated with a double band of waves, one of the most typical motifs of Peruvian traditional iconography (Maahun, Trujillo).

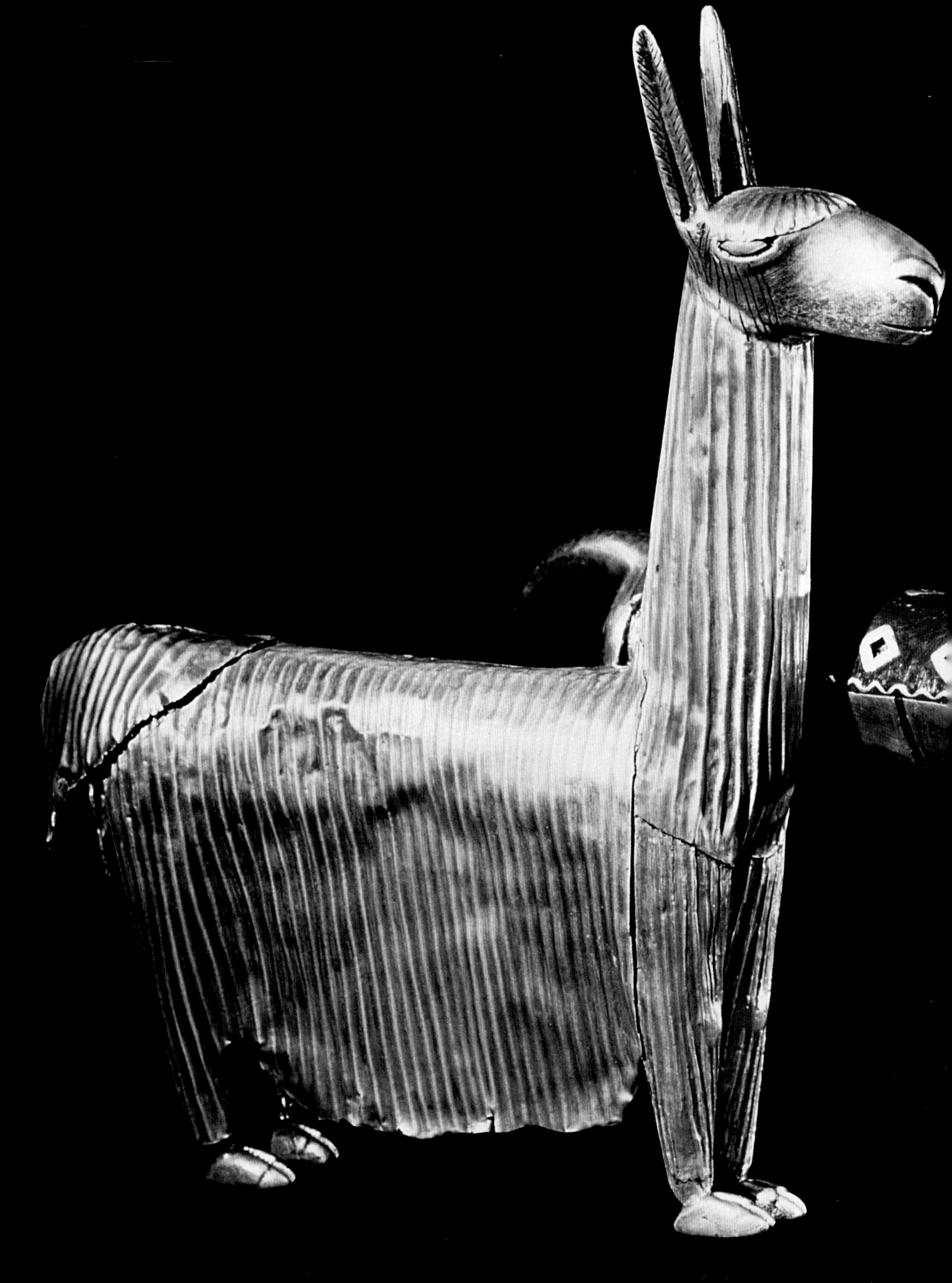

20-21 - In this Inca depiction of silver miniatures (15th-16th centuries) a woman is accompanied by two llamas. Llamas were used for their wool, for carrying goods, and for their meat (American Museum of Natural History, New York).

EARLY CUZCO VALLEY SOCIETIES

Very recent archaeological investigations carried out in the Cuzco Valley have shed light on the history of the area before the Inca civilization. Now we know that the first groups of hunter-gatherers were in the area 10,000 years BC. These groups were small bands which made occasional use of local resources but did not permanently inhabit the area, as indicated by the tools made with imported stone that have been found by archaeologists. We have to wait until the 4th millennium BC to find the first evidence of stone-carved tools associated with permanent settlements; these are the very common "guide fossils" that map the presence of prehistoric hunter-gatherers.

The period between the 2nd millennium and the second century BC was defined with a more general term as the Formative Period, which also describes the roughly contemporary phases of other Andean areas. Although on the Peruvian coast the Formative Period is well-known thanks to the study of the numerous monumental ceremonial sites (such as Cerro Sechin and Chavín de Huántar) carried out in the last 50 years, the Formative period in the Cuzco area is far less well-known. We know that permanent settlements were consolidated, the most important of which may have represented the

chief villages in a system of small lordships. It was thought that this differentiation between more or less important settlements may have developed in parallel with the growing differentetiation of individuals into social classes. Also associated with this phenomenon is the production of sumptuary goods, the privileged expression of the economic power of the small aristocratic elite. The beginning of the Formative Period also coincides with the onset of ceramic production.

Throughout the whole Peruvian territory, the first half of the 1st millennium AD marked a period of great fervor: in many human groups there was an increase in settlements and in population, with a more intensive occupation of the land. In this phase there were many technological innovations and the arts developed greatly. In the Cuzco area, there is nothing comparable to the great realms of the Peruvian coast, though from the few studies conducted on this era one gleans that it was a period of general growth, in part thanks to more systematic agricultural practices based on the construction of irrigation channels. The settlements in this phase are concentrated in the most accessible part of the Cuzco Valley, i.e., the southwestern area bounded by the Huatanay River. The most common pottery items of this period were well baked with a

cream and white engobe with polychromatic geometrical designs; the type is known as *Qotakalli* pottery. Evidence of exotic pottery has led to the supposition that the small lordships of the Cuzco Valley, even though they remained within that region, had relations with other regions, especially in the area of the southern plateau where great civilizations had also developed with settlements such as Pucara and Tiwanaku on the shores of Lake Titicaca. We will see the importance of these ancient contacts, bearing in mind that the area of Lake Titicaca was considered by the Incas as one of the mythical places related to the creation of their race.

22 and 23 bottom - The outer platform of Cerro Sechín (Casma Valley) was covered by 400 steles with reliefs of armed figures and dismembered bodies (15th century BC).

22-23 - Cerro Sechín was one of the most significant monumental complexes of the Formative Period (15th century BC).

23 top and the center - The access stairway on the platform of Cerro Sechín was decorated with polychromatic friezes.

24 - This stirrup jug (10 inches/25.5 cm in height), an example of Cupisnique manufacture (11th-4th centuries BC) was produced on the north coast of Peru. It develops a typical figurative theme of Chavín, such as the engraved cat on the object's belly (Maahun, Trujillo).

25 left - This Cupisnique stirrup jug depicts a man carrying a llama on his shoulders (Enrico Poli Collection, Lima).

25 right - The jug/scupture (16.1 inches/41 cm in height) depicts a loin-clothed figure carrying a load on his shoulders. It dates back to the Viru-Gallinazo culture (8th to 2nd centuries BC) (Larco Herrera Museum, Cuzco).

PRE-INCA CHRONOLOGY AND CULTURES

Studies made in the last fifty years have shown that there were complex cultures in Peru which had already developed in the country's coastal area during the 3rd millennium BC. But this knowledge of such varied cultural manifestations of the Peruvian peoples arrived too late to influence substantively the study of Peruvian archaeology. In the past, it was thought that only from the 1st millennium BC did super-regional cultures emerge. We have already spoken of the "master sequence" of the Andean area, i.e., a relative chronology which began with the observation of changes that took place from the second half of the 1st millennium BC in the small Ica Valley in the southern Peruvian coast. For the previous period, the master sequence was based on the observation of other cultural macro-phenomena such as the establishment of what was considered the mother culture of Peruvian civilizations, i.e., the Chavín culture (from the archaeological site of the same name in the heart of the central sierra).

The master sequence begins with the Chavín culture (better defined today as a tradition shared by different human groups). As it was believed that the Chavín culture had extended its influence on other parts of the Andes, it was long thought of as a unifying culture; the period in which the site was active was identified as a single cultural horizon (the so-called Ancient Horizon, 1000-200 BC).

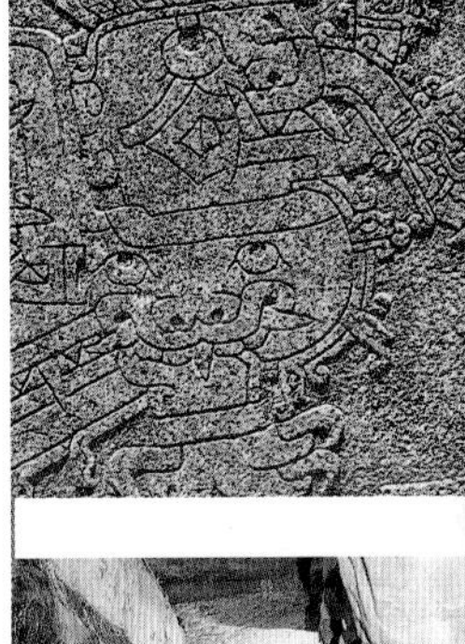

26 left and 26-27 - The so-called *Castillo* is a temple built in the last phase of the Ceremonial center of Chavín De Huantar (12th-2nd centuries). During the formative period, the collapsed quadrangular plaza opposite was probably the site of important religious ceremonies.

26 bottom - On the *Castillo*'s western walls one can admire the so-called nail-heads which represent the faces of the temple's priests and Shamans.

27 top - This architrave with a frieze of monstrous eagles decorated the Templo Nuevo's door (New Temple) in Chavín, and developed the figurative themes of the Chavín temple.

27 bottom - Beneath Chavín de Huantar's platforms lies a network of galleries used as waterways and as depositories for the ceremonial center's offerings.

28 - This clay figurine, with paint applied after firing, comes from Peru's North Coast Tembladera culture (Jequetepeque), contemporary with the Chavín culture, 8th to 4th centuries (Enrico Poli Collection, Lima).

29 left - A stirrup vase decorated with a frieze of trophy heads, probably made on the North Coast of Peru during the Ancient Horizon Period (12th-2nd centuries) (Amano Museum, Lima)

29 right - The Raimondi Stele (76.7 inches/195 cm in height) depicts one of the supreme deities of the Chavín temple. It was discovered near the temple by the famous Italian explorer Antonio Raimondi, and dates to the final phase of this culture, the 11th-14th centuries (Museo Nacional de Arqueología, Antropología e Historia del Perú, Lima).

30 - This gold ruff (4.8 inches/12.3 cm in diameter), decorated with a monstrous figure, dates to the Chavín culture (Dumbarton Oaks Collection, Washington, D.C.).

30-31 - This pendent (4 inches/10.4 cm in length) depicts a cat's profile. representation of the cat is common in Chavín culture (Dumbarton Oaks Collection, Washington, D.C.).

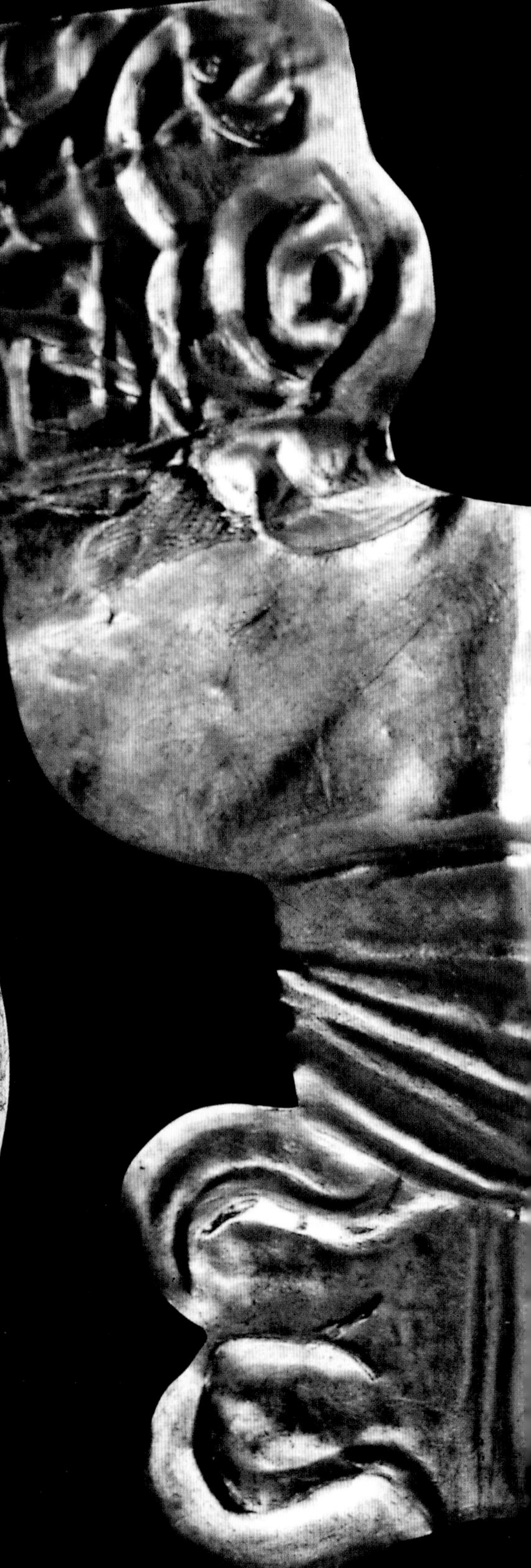

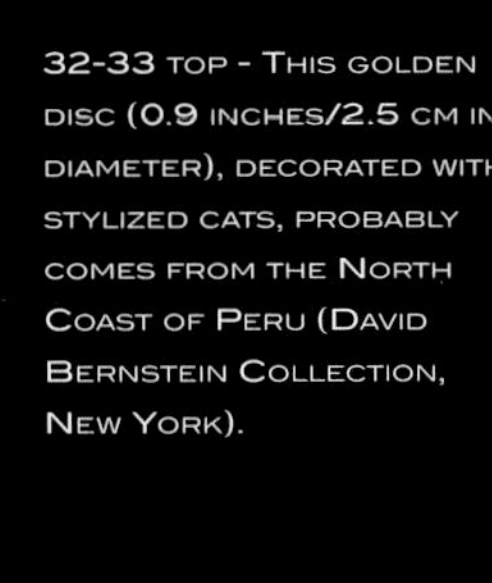

32-33 top - This golden disc (0.9 inches/2.5 cm in diameter), decorated with stylized cats, probably comes from the North Coast of Peru (David Bernstein Collection, New York).

32-33 bottom - This gold pendent (1.9 inches/5 cm in height) portrays a sitting cat. The animal's features reflect typical Chavínoid figurative forms (David Bernstein collection, New York).

33 left - This gold plate (4.8 inches/ 12.3 cm in diameter) represents Chavín de Huantar's principal deity but was found in Lambayeque region (Dumbarton Oaks Collection, Washington, D.C.).

33 right - This ritual teaspoon (4.3 inches/11.1 cm in length), discovered in Chavín de Huantar, was probably used for the inhalation of hallucinogens during religious ceremonies. The figure on the edge, with an eagle tattooed on his shoulder, is thought to be a shaman (Dumbarton Oaks Collection, Washington, D.C.).

The following phase was defined through the observation of another time-defined phenomenon, the appearance of different regional styles of pottery in the northern Peruvian coast. This era saw different cultures emerge, such as the Moche and Nazca on the coast and the Recuay in the Central Cordillera. For this reason it was defined as the Intermediate Ancient Period, AD 0-600, in contrast with the term "horizon" which defined a phase in which there was only one important culture. The Moche were the best known culture in the Intermediate Ancient Period, with settlements covering a very vast area of the central-southern Peruvian coast from AD 0 to 800. Today it is thought that there were at least two centers of power, one farther north (where lies a pyramid, the Huaca Rajada, in which several lords' tombs like the one of the so-called Lord of Sipán have been found) and the other farther south: these were flourishing settlements which hosted a growing population and ever more specialized artisans making pottery and working gold. Moche artistic representations not only portray the religious caste and the divinities, but also a new elite of lords who loved being portrayed with symbols of economic and religious power. The first representations of human figures and of architecturally well-defined settlements are indicators that have led specialists to think that this was the time in which the germs of a state organization within the Andes began. This period is also characterized by the great liveliness of the arts, which developed numerous innovative techniques. Moche pottery is characterized by the use of bivalve casts and a fine cream color engobing. Fictile production was along two main branches: (1) portrait pottery, with completely modeled figures representing people from daily life as well as figure animals, fruit, plants, divinities and prisoners of war (the whole period is characterized by numerous conflicts and ethnic fighting), and (2) ceramics with fine lines where mythological scenes are represented, such as divinities or hunting scenes tied to rituals.

35 - These golden pincers (6.8 inches/17.5 cm long) are decorated with a face and two crested dragons, mythical animals which often represent deities in Peru's North Coast region (Vicus culture; 3rd century BC - 5th century AD) (Bruning Museum, Lambayeque).

36-37 - This embossed gold head or chest ornament of the Vicus culture depicts a creature with feline attributes (Museo Nacional de Arqueología, Antropología e Historia del Perú, Lima).

38-39 - The murals of Huaca de la Luna, one of the Moche ceremonial centers.

34-35 - The copper and gold funerary mask (7.8 inches/20 cm in height) from tomb 2 of the Dos Cabeza archaeological site is one of the most spectacular finds of recent years: it probably covered the face of a Moche sovereign (1st – 8th centuries AD) (Museo de sitio de Chan Chan, Trujillo).

40-41 - The Huaca de la Luna murals depict the deities of the Moche temples. In this case a variant of the figure of the "Decapitator" god, often shown with a knife in hand in the process of performing sacrifices.

41 - In addition to deities, some Moche murals also portrayed animals, as in the case of this stylized ray fish originating from Huaca de la Luna.

42 - A Moche warrior is depicted in this terracotta jug (1st-8th centuries AD) in the typical kneeling position and with a conical-pointed staff (Maahun, Trujillo).

43 - The Moche stirrup jug is surmounted by the figure of a man with clasped hands. This pose, together with the scars that mark his face, probably identifies him as a priest or a shaman (Maahun, Trujillo).

44 - This depiction of the animal world, as shown in this frog-shaped jug, recalls the sacredness of the natural world in Moche culture (Maahun, Trujillo).

45 top - The jug (5.5 inches/14 cm in height) depicts a warrior goose. It was discovered in the tomb of a Moche priest in Huaco de la Luna and represents perhaps the transfiguration of the dead person into his animal alter ego (Maahun, Trujillo).

45 bottom - Often the Moche deities recall the animal world, as shown in this depiction of the crab-god with human and feline attributes (Maahun, Trujillo).

46 left - The depiction of skeletons in the act of playing an instrument or some other activity was common among the Moche. In this way the imporance of death in the human life cycle was emphasized (Maahun, Trujillo).

46 right - This Moche vase depicts a warrior with a Recuay headdress (Private collection).

47 - The expressivity of Moche vases makes one think of actual portraits (Maahun, Trujillo).

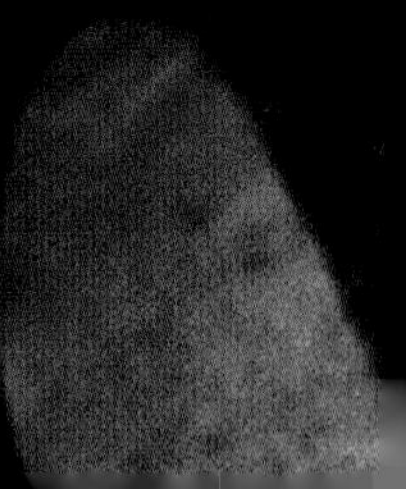

48 - In Moche culture, prisoners are depicted in consistent ways, such as naked, their hands bound behind their backs, and often with a rope around their neck (Maahun, Trujillo).

49 - The Moche jug represents a figure with the typical facial features of the dead: the nose cartilages are emphasized and the lips are curled back to show the teeth (Maahun, Trujillo).

50 TOP - THE PAIR OF MOCHE EARRINGS IN GOLD AND TURQUOISE MOSAIC REPRESENTS SOME WARRIORS WITH BIRD ATTRIBUTES; THEY ARE HOLDING A SLING AND A POINTED STAFF (LARCO HERRERA MUSEUM, LIMA).

50 bottom - Moche earrings decorated with a frieze of lizards (Larco Herrera Museum, Lima).

51 - This Moche earring depicts a figure holding a trophy head (Gold museum, Lima).

52 - This effigy of deities with feline attributes (22 inches/56 cm in height) belongs to the funerary offerings of the Lord of Sipán. These images evoked the sovereign's role of mediator with the supernatural world (Museo Tumbas Reales de Sipan, Lambayeque).

53 top - An open-armed figure (27.5 inches/70 cm long) is the principal element of this ornament found in the treasure that accompanied the body of the Lord of Sipán as a symbol of rank (Museo Tumbas Reales de Sipán, Lambayeque).

53 bottom - This gilded bronze feline head, together with similar others, was part of a necklace discovered in the tomb of the Lord of Sipán. The animal's teeth are made from fragments of shells (David Bernstein Collection, New York).

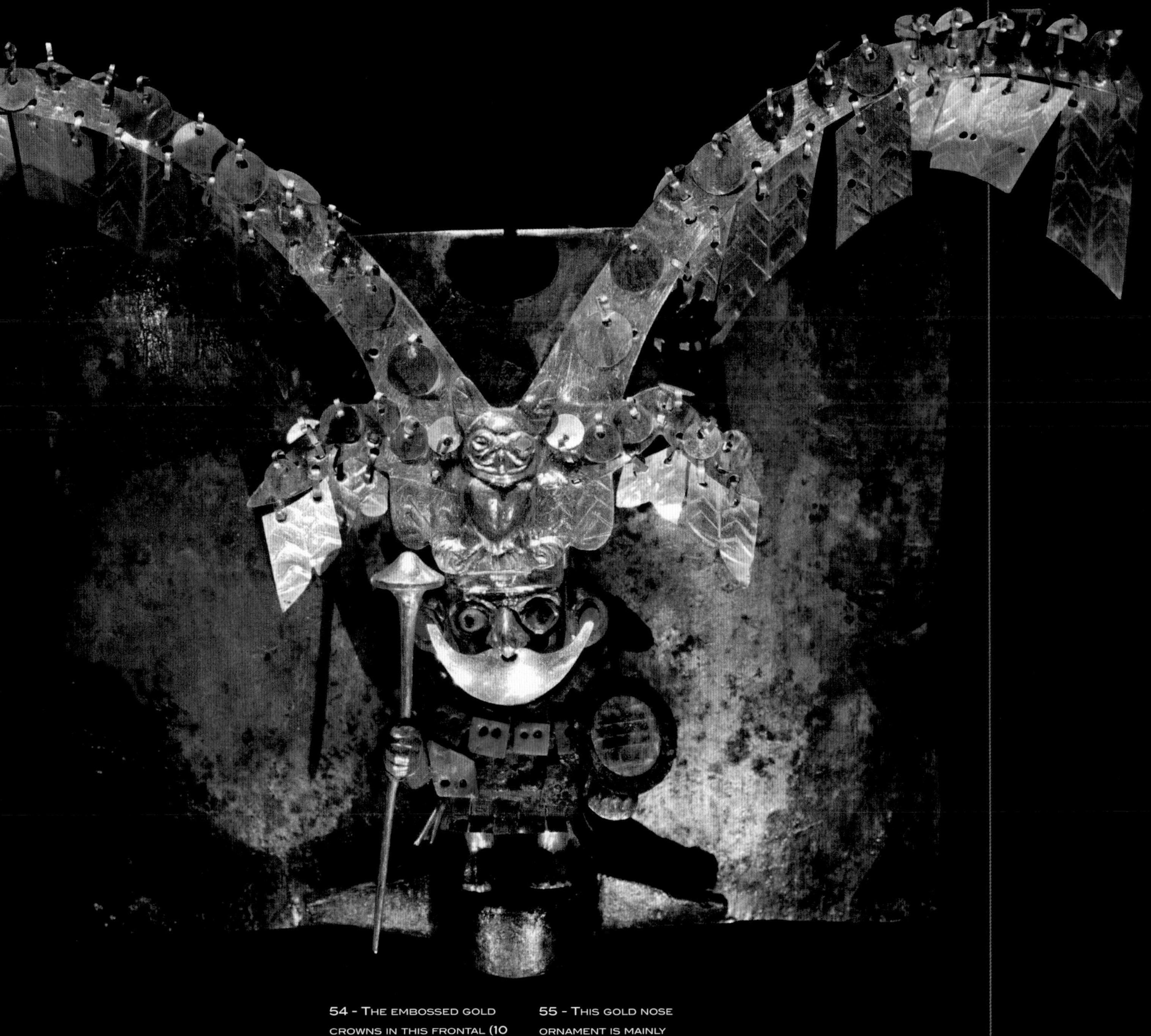

54 - The embossed gold crowns in this frontal (10 inches/25.6 cm in height) depict the head of a cat with two birds (top) and a human face with two crested cats (below) (Larco Herrera Museum, Lima).

55 - This gold nose ornament is mainly decorated with the figure of a sovereign, probably the Old Lord of Sipán (Museo Tumbas Reales de Sipán, Lambayeque).

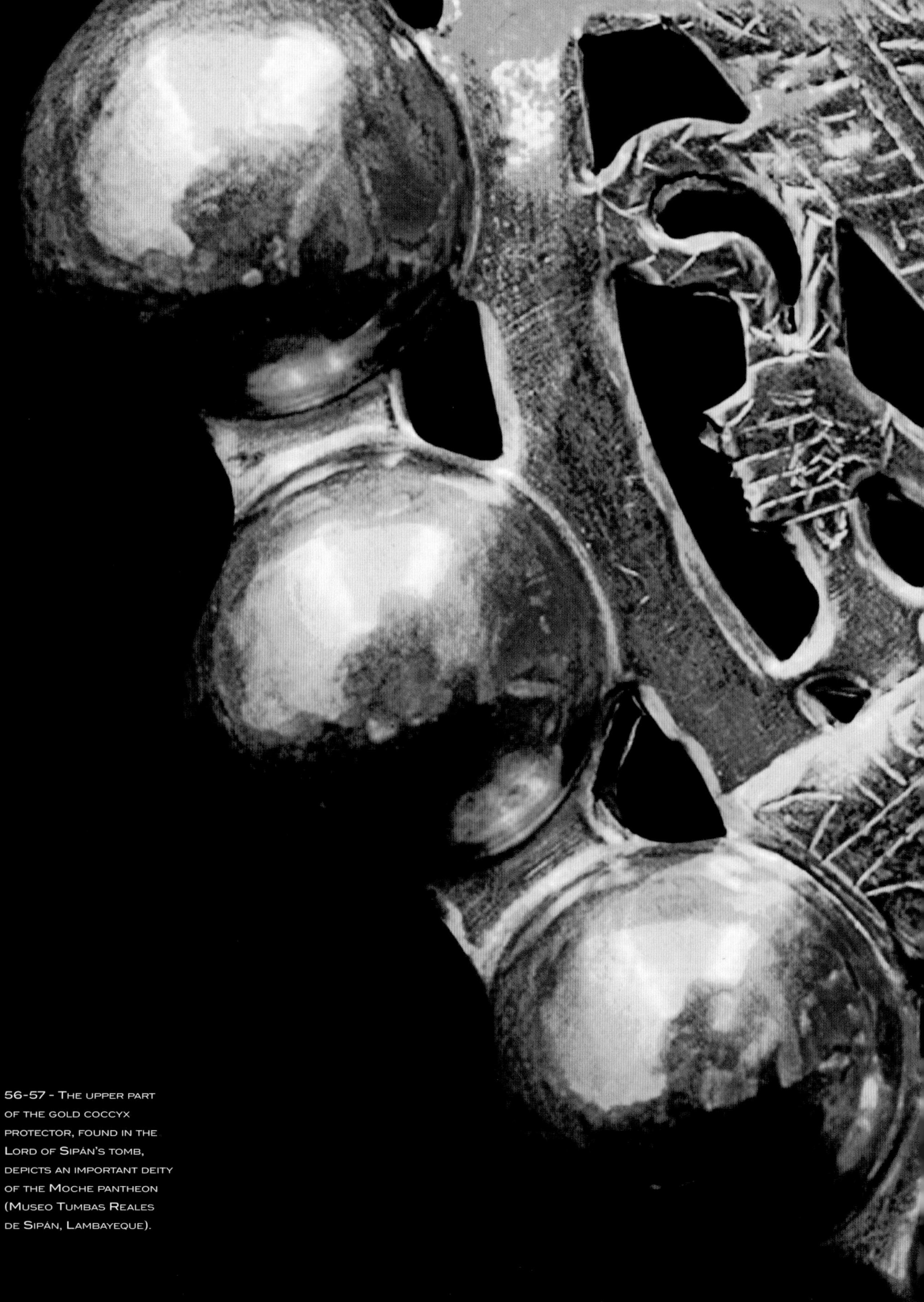

56-57 - The upper part of the gold coccyx protector, found in the Lord of Sipán's tomb, depicts an important deity of the Moche pantheon (Museo Tumbas Reales de Sipán, Lambayeque).

58-59 - The male head was part of a necklace of the Moche Lord of Sipán (Museo Tumbas Reales de Sipán, Lambayeque).

59 top left - The axe-shaped gold coccyx protector (17.7 inces/45 cm in height) was found under the body of the Lord of Sipán (Museo Tumbas Reales de Sipán, Lambayeque).

59 top right - On the sceptre found in the Lord of Sipán's tomb is depicted a lord in the process of striking an enemy (Museo Tumbas Reales de Sipán, Lambayeque).

59 bottom - A reconstruction of the Lord of Sipán's burial.

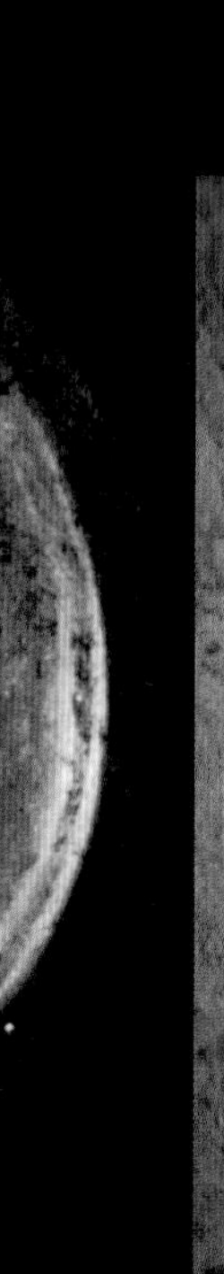

60 top - The Nazca (1st century BC-7th century AD), the most important cultural tradition of the southern coast of Peru during the Ancient Intermediate Period, built imposing ceremonial centers and incised geometric and figurative lines.

60 bottom - The terrain of the Pampa of Nazca has numerous incised designs. Their whose lines probably served to indicate ritual paths or acted as signs which in some way indicated water sources.

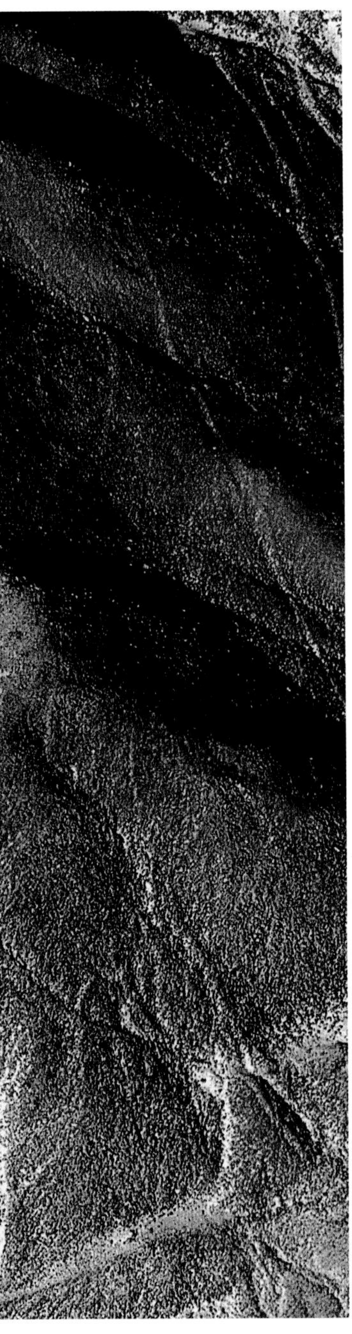

At the same time as the development of the Moche culture, the Nazca culture was developing in the southern coastal area of Peru. The most impressive remains are certainly those of the Cahuachi ceremonial center, which occupied more than 1200 acres (485 hectares) with its complex of pyramids, temples and squares. The ceremonial center was the source of the driving force for economic activity and political and religious power. It was also connected to the famous lines in the desert, extensive geoglyphs on an ample territory; they represent the magical religious world of the Nazca. These drawings in the desert were made to be seen from afar, and they are sometimes enormous (some figurative ones are up to 600 ft/182 m) across while the geometrical ones extend over 5.5 miles/8.85 km). The Nazca geoglyphs were undoubtedly made by shift work that involved the whole community. This method clearly explains the Andean "manner" of understanding religion: tracing and then maintaining the visibility of these lines, which were perhaps ritual routes (or, as some hypothesize, visual markers of water sources), was a moment of reinforcement of social identity strictly tied to the territory and the sacred landscape.

Nazca art developed in two distinct phases, one called "monumental" and the other called "proliferous." In the monumental phase in most cases terrifying divinities were represented, often zoomorphic in aspect, like the so-called flying monster. The human figure became progressively more often represented even though it never became preponderant. In the final phase of the Nazca culture, a geometrization and extreme stylization of figurative themes prevailed, populating the representations in the style known as "proliferous."

The Intermediate Ancient Period was followed by another "unifying" period, that of the so-called Huari culture (AD 600-1000), and then another phase of regionalism (Recent Intermediate Period, AD 1000-1400), and finally the Late Horizon or Inca (AD 1400-1532).

Given the current state of knowledge this "master sequence," now historicized, appears with many limitations: today it is no longer thought, in fact, that the protagonists of the historical phases defined as Horizons (i.e. the Ancient Horizon or Chavín, the Middle Horizon or Huari and the Late Horizon or Inca) ever really governed the whole Peruvian territory, neither is it thought that regional traditions worked only during the so-called Intermediate Periods. The relative chronology of Peru is far more intricate than it was thought to be until a few decades ago. This recognition, as we will shortly see, is thanks to the genuine revolutions brought about by recent archaeological discoveries.

60-61 - This stylized human figure, erroneously defined as "the extraterrestrial", effectively represents Nazca art's tendency toward abstraction, which is also noted in other artistic manifestations.

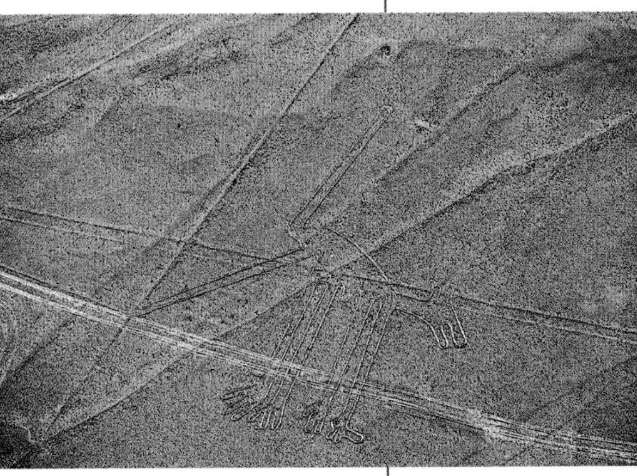

61 - The figurative themes of the Nazca lines devloped onthe motifs present on pottery; they portray the animal and natural world. Top, the shape of a spider is reproduced by lines; below, the form of a dog can be recognized.

62 TOP - REPRESENTATIONS OF THE FEMALE APPEAR IN THE LATE PHASE OF NAZCA ART (MAAHUN, TRUJILLO).

62 BOTTOM LEFT - THE TYPE OF VASE CALLED *FLORERO* (9 INCHES/23 CM IN HEIGHT) IS COMMON IN NAZCA ART. THE HEAD IS REPRESENTED BOTH AS A TROPHY AND AS A PORTRAIT (BRITISH MUSEUM, LONDON).

62 BOTTOM RIGHT - THIS STIRRUP SPOUTED VASE PORTRAYS AN ANTHROMORPHOUS MYTHICAL BEING WHICH FORMS PART OF THE NAZCA PANTHEON (MUSEO NACIONAL DE ARQUEOLOGÍA, ANTROPOLOGÍA E HISTORIA DEL PERÚ, LIMA).

63 - THIS NAZCA VASE PORTRAYS A DIGNITARY WITH FACIAL PAINT (CERAMIC MUSEUM, SÈVRES).

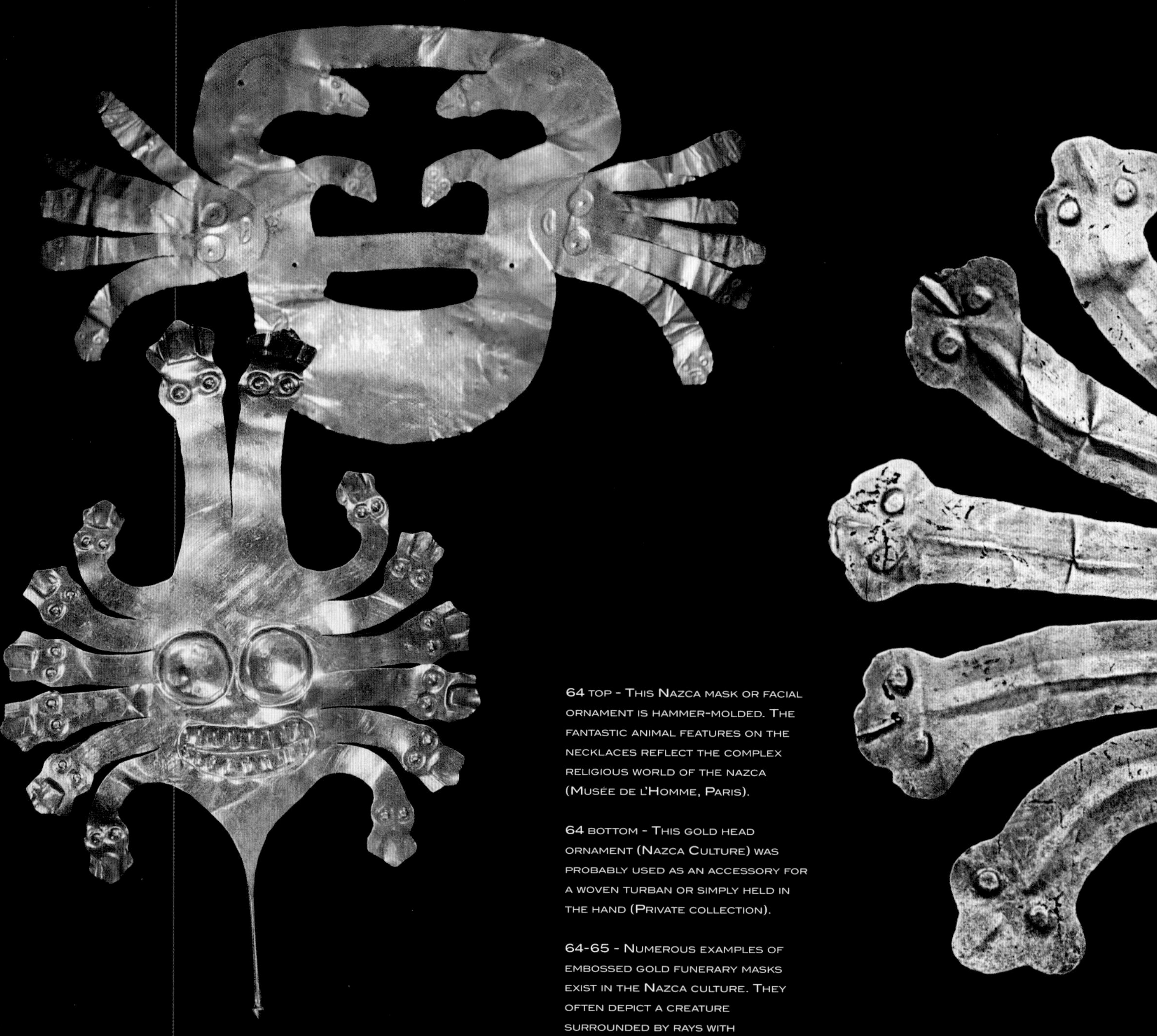

64 TOP - THIS NAZCA MASK OR FACIAL ORNAMENT IS HAMMER-MOLDED. THE FANTASTIC ANIMAL FEATURES ON THE NECKLACES REFLECT THE COMPLEX RELIGIOUS WORLD OF THE NAZCA (MUSÉE DE L'HOMME, PARIS).

64 BOTTOM - THIS GOLD HEAD ORNAMENT (NAZCA CULTURE) WAS PROBABLY USED AS AN ACCESSORY FOR A WOVEN TURBAN OR SIMPLY HELD IN THE HAND (PRIVATE COLLECTION).

64-65 - NUMEROUS EXAMPLES OF EMBOSSED GOLD FUNERARY MASKS EXIST IN THE NAZCA CULTURE. THEY OFTEN DEPICT A CREATURE SURROUNDED BY RAYS WITH ZOOMORPHIC LIMBS (MUSÉE DE L'HOMME, PARIS).

66 top left - The cultural tradition of the Recuay developed during the Ancient Intermediate Period (0-600 AD). The Recuay elite were the predominant subjects of these stone and terracotta portraits (35 inches/ 89 cm in height) (Museo Arqueológico de Huaraz).

66 top right - Recuay stone sculptures often decorated the walls of buildings as in the case of this feline head (27.1 inches/69 cm long), an animal often represented in Recuay iconography (Museo Arqueológico de Huaraz).

66-67 - The figure is depicted in the stone architrave (66.1 inches/168 cm long) is holding some trophy heads in his hands and is accompanied by two cats (Museo Arqueológico de Huaraz).

67 top left - The use of the tenon heads (14.9 inches/38 cm in height) dates back to the Chavín era and continued during the Recuay period (Maahun, Trujillo).

67 top right - This head (22.8 inches/58 cm in height), probably part of a statue, is rounded and flat nosed, can be traced back to Recuay culture lithic production from the Huaraz region (Museo Arqueológico de Huaraz).

THE HUARI IN THE CUZCO VALLEY

Around AD 500 an aggressive people coming from the center-southern Andes, from the Ayacucho sierra north of Cuzco, was expanding its influence to some crucial areas of what is now Peruvian territory. The most visible sign of its diffusion is the spread of a typical ceramic style and a chessboard city model designed on the shape of the capital, the settlement of Huari, which, with its 20,000 to 30,000 inhabitants, was one of the most important of its time. The origin of this city idea, which many consider the first truly Andean city, may have come once again from the South, from the cultural tradition of the plateau area: the cells which make up the orthogonal structures, with D-shaped patios, are similar to those observed in the Pucara site (200 BC – AD 200/400), in the Titicaca basin.

The Huaris were particularly important for the history of the Andes because they were the first power that went beyond its regional confines and had contacts, if not a presence, in a vast territory which extended from the area of the Huatanay River (where they built the city of Pikillacta) to a few miles from Cuzco.

68 BOTTOM RIGHT - THE JUG WITH RELIEFS PORTRAYS A HIGH DIGNITARY OF THE HUARI CULTURE. THE CENTRAL THEME DEPICTS THE SO-CALLED STAFF GOD (LARCO HERRERA MUSEUM, LIMA).

69 - THIS HUARI TAPESTRY DEPICTS A FANTASTIC BEING (MUSEO NACIONAL DE ARQUEOLOGÍA, ANTROPOLOGÍA E HISTORIA DEL PERÚ, LIMA).

68 TOP RIGHT AND BOTTOM LEFT - UPON THE TWO PAIRS OF HUARI EARRINGS MADE FROM TESSERAE OF HARD STONE, THE HEADS OF BIRDS OF PREY AND FELINES ARE DEPICTED AS WELL AS ABSTRACT GEOMETRIC ELEMENTS (PRIVATE COLLECTION).

During the Huari era some cultural tools were developed which the Inca were to use thereafter. One example is the road system, very useful for trade routes on which ideas and products traveled. This phase of the Peruvian history is characterized by another cultural phenomenon of great importance, that of the assertion of the important ceremonial center of Tiwanaku. Tiwanaku was a strongly symbolic place, a mythical land of origin transformed into a sanctuary by the local populations, as its original name seems to indicate (*Taypikala*, or "the stone in the center" in the ancient local Aymara language). It was also a multiethnic economic and trade power, which soon clashed with the southward expansion of the Huari.

The interaction between the two powers took place at the turn of the 5th century AD, on the southern Peruvian coast, in the Moquegua Valley, where groups tied respectively to the Huari and the Tiwanaku occupied different parts of the valley. Burials

with mixed ceramic trousseaux, which belong to both cultural traditions, led to the belief that relations were not too problematic, at least in this area.

The interaction between the two civilizations is also evident from the "loan" of some images of divinities which the Huari adapted from the religious tradition of the plateau area, which reached its maximum extension with the religious sculpture of the Tiwanaku temple: for example, the iconography of the so-called "god of sticks" which appears on the Gateway to the Sun.

While some administrative structures that were to greatly facilitate the Inca expansion in the Peruvian territory 400 years later were inherited from the Huari, Tiwanaku provided the ideological basis for the expansion of the empire. Tiwanaku was in fact considered a mythical place of creation and the center of a political and economic power that was placed there by divine will, and maintained by sovereigns also held to be of divinie descent.

It is not by chance, as we will soon see, that the Cuzco people located themselves in the Titicaca area, a *pacarina*, or place of origin of their race. So if the prestige ofTiwanaku was still alive in

Inca times, the Huari presence was more time-limited but more incisive. Not only did they build the important site of Pikillacta (in the Cuzco area), but they imported ceramics of Ayacuchana origin which have been found in different archaeological sites in the Huatanay Valley. Furthermore, the prestige of the Huari must have been noteworthy since the local artisans imitated them for so long. In fact, for quite some time they continued to produce *qotakalli* pottery, imitating the most classical styles of Huari ceramics, giving life to a curious mix.

70 TOP - KALASASAYA'S OUTER WALLS IN TIWANAKU, ENCLOSED LARGE OPEN SQUARES FOR GATHERINGS OF THE FAITFUL.

70 BOTTOM - THE STONE STATUE (15.7 INCHES/40 CM IN HEIGHT) OF A FIGURE WITH A HEADDRESS IN THE SHAPE OF A STAIR-STEP BELONGS TO THE OLDEST PHASE OF THE TIWANAKU CULTURE AND HAS WAS FOUND IN THE CUZCO REGION (ETHNOLOGISCHES MUSEUM, BERLIN).

70-71 - KALASASAYA TEMPLE'S STAIRCASE LEADS TO THE PONCE MONOLITH, A SCULPTURE WHICH PERHAPS REPRESENTS ONE OF THE SACRED CITY'S SOVEREIGNS.

71 BOTTOM LEFT - THE 15TH STELE OF THE SEMI-SUBTERRANEAN TEMPLE OF TIWANAKU DEPICTS A BEARDED FIGURE.

71 BOTTOM RIGHT - "NAIL-HEADS" WERE INSTALLED IN THE SQUARE OF THE SEMI-SUBTERRANEAN TEMPLE OF TIWANAKU.

72 TOP - PIKILLACTA'S STREETS, ENCLOSED BY WALLS OVER 6.5 FT (2 M) HIGH, ALLOWED CIRCULATION BETWEEN THE DIFFERENT SECTORS OF THE CITY, BUILT IN SEPARATE SECTIONS, IN TYPICAL HUARI STRUCTURAL STYLE.

72 BOTTOM - THE CIRCULAR STRUCTURE IN PIKILLACTA (PROBABLY A STORAGE CENTER) FUNCTIONED AS AN OUTPOST DEIGNED TO PROMOTE EXPLOITATION OF THE REGION'S AGRICULTURAL POTENTIAL.

72-73 - THE AERIAL VIEW OF PIKILLACTA IN THE CUZCO REGION CLEARLY PRESENTS THE ORTHOGONAL CELLED STRUCTURE OF THE HUARI CULTURE.

73 BOTTOM LEFT - THIS BOWL WITH A FLARED EDGE DECORATED WITH GEOMETRICAL MOTIFS INTERPRETS THE CLASSIC TIWANAKU POLYCHROMY, WHICH USES A RICH PALETTE OF COLORS (MUSEO NACIONAL DE ARQUEOLOGÍA, LA PAZ, BOLIVIA).

One of the most impressive Huari architectural projects, and certainly the most eye-catching sign of their presence in the Cuzco area was the Pikillacta settlement.

Conceived, built, inhabited and abandoned within fewer than 300 years, Pikillacta has an orthogonal plan, with cells defined by high walls that still stand in some buildings and are over 10 ft (3 m) tall. Even though the Huari probably used local labor for its construction, organized in shifts, the general design of the site betrays a project that has nothing to do with local tradition. This also explains the fact that the site was inhabited for a relatively short period, with some parts still under construction when it was abandoned. But why did the Huari undertake such an ambitious project in the specific area of Cuzco? Some researchers think that this area was ideal to develop a province to be used intensively for agricultural products: the local lordships in fact still had not occupied the whole territory by the second half of the 1st millennium AD. Pikillacta was built in an area where there were no settlements from the *Qotokalli* period (the Lucre basin, 20 miles/32 km south of Cuzco), an area which was still little used and which the Huari transformed with imposing terraces and canals.

The construction of a great southern capital, which was to serve as a granary (there is a whole neighborhood of silos in the settlement) for the growth of Huari power may not have worked according to plan: at the end of the 1st millennium AD the site stopped being used. The layers found there yield evidence of fire and the burial of structures. This indicates that toward the end of the life of the site there were clashes between its residents and local populations.

The ephemeral Huari presence constituted an important milestone for the development of the Huatanay area: from the ashes of Pikillacta local ethnic groups emerged, destined to cross the Inca power with some Huari innovations which had been absorbed by locals. Perhaps the most evident sign of a new tradition which summed up past and present can be appreciated in the mixed style of the pottery born in this phase, which was to provide a repertory of form and decorations for the *Killke* art, the early period of Inca emergence.

73 BOTTOM RIGHT - THIS JUG DEPICTS A HIGH-RANKING FIGURE WITH A ROBE DECORATED IN THE TIE-DYE TECHNIQUE, COMMON ALONG THE SOUTHERN COAST OF PERU. IT PROVIDES EVIDENCE OF THE DIFFUSION OF THE HUARI CULTURE BEYOND THE CENTRAL ANDES (MUSEO NACIONAL DE ARQUEOLOGÍA, ANTROPOLOGÍA E HISTORIA DEL PERÚ, LIMA).

MANCO CAPAC AND HIS BROTHERS

The most evident sign of the decline of the Huari power noted by archaeologists is the dominance of a style in pottery known as *Killke*. This heralds in form and some decorative stylistic elements the work of the Incas. It has long been thought that this style represents the oldest phase of Inca pottery, in the period between the 11th and 15th centuries AD. Cuzco, centre of the Tawantinsuyu which the tradition says was founded by the first Inca, the mythical Manco Capac (the word "Inca" is used to mean both the people and its divine sovereign), is where most of this work is found and archaeologists have mapped a capillary distribution of it there. It is difficult to estimate the exact extension of Cuzco in the *Killke* era, and the pottery was not limited to the capital. In this phase, in fact, there was great activity in the construction of sites, agricultural terraces, and the occupation of new territories. Starting from AD 1000 these ceramics become very widespread, leading researchers to suppose that the tradition was shared among different regional ethnic groups cited in the chronicles. Among these groups emerged the peoples which we now call the Incas. Over the course of three centuries they came to dominate most of the peoples in the Cuzco area.

The first Inca sovereigns also apparently ruled at that time; their names have been communicated to us by the surviving chronicles. They carried out an unscrupulous marriage policy to ensure they had the support of rather powerful groups such as the Ayarmaca. According to the noted historian María Rostworowski, the Ayarmaca played a fundamental role in the foundation of Cuzco: with their alliance a group so strong was to emerge that it became the main power in the Huatanay area. The same researcher holds that one of the most important Cuzco foundation myths, that of four Ayar brothers, in fact alludes to the Ayarmaca. Their creation myth appears to pre-empt a stratagem invented by the Inca to give, in mythological history, continuity between their group and that of the local ethnic group which was originally more important. In the struggle foorsupremacy, the Incas emerged as a group managing to give political stability to the area. The official Inca historiography, as we will see, recounts a rather different story: that of a group of chosen men and women of divine ancestry who came from afar to conquer a promised land, the Cuzco Valley. Spanish chroniclers who heard these myths of origin took advantage of them in order to present Inca history as that of a dynastic monarchy of European type, so as to more easily replace the ruling power. There are numerous myths recounting the beginning of the royal Inca stock and how they reached to Cuzco area. Notwithstanding the relevant differences, there are many common basic elements that allude to the occupation of the land and the incorporation of local groups. Among these one of the most suggestive is that told by the chronicler Santacruz Pachacuti: it tells of how in Tiwanaku the sun, moon, stars and humanity (the Inca) were created, forged out of stone. The people, starting from the sacred city of Tiwanaku then populated the world. The bond with Tiwanaku and the area of Lake Titicaca is not casual: for a long time historians thought Tiwanaku was an important ceremonial center. Instead, it

74 - In this famous colonial-era table (1709-99), with clearly visible detail, depicts Manco Capac, founding father of the Inca dynasty (Pedro de Osma Museum, Lima).

75 - The depiction of Mama Ocllo, spouse of Manco Capac, the first great Inca symmetrically completes the presentation of the first Inca dynasty (Pedro de Osma Museum, Lima).

was a real, city covering 2.3 sq. miles (6 sq. km) with a population of between 30,000 and 50,000 people. But Taypikala, as it used to be called, was not only the headquarters of the Tiwanaku political elite, but more specifically the center of a symbolical world, the materialization on earth of a cosmic order and its divinities. For this reason the holy city was the ideal place for numerous creation myths to be set, and not only by the Aymara-speaking peoples dwelling on the shores of Lake Titicaca. Obviously it was in the Incas' interest to associate themselves with such a strong tradition, to the extent that it was much visited during their supremacy as an important place of worship.

Even the chronicler Garcilaso de la Vega indicated the Titicaca area as a place of origin from which the first Inca divine couple arose (Manco Capac and Mama Ocllo), created by the god Viracocha. From the South they went to Cuzco where they made their home by planting a vara (stick) in the ground, symbolically fertilizing it.

Juan de Betanzos in *Suma y narración de los Incas* (1551) instead lists Manco Capac as one of the four brothers who emerged from a mythical place of creation (or *pacarina* in Quechua, the Inca language): this might have been a grotto known as Tambotoco near Pacaritambo (about 20 miles/32 km from Cuzco). Bringing agricultural products which were to be the basis of the Inca economy from this sort of "laboratory of life" from which he emerged together with his brothers (the Ayar) and their relative wives/sisters, Manco Capac managed to reach Cuzco, where he established himself, marking the borders of his territory by turning one of his brothers into stone. In all the myths the special origin of the Inca is underlined, implying a divine investiture (implicit or direct) of a divine power. This provided them with a sort of metaphysical justification to establish themselves as sovereigns in the land of Cuzco.

According to the researcher Franklin Pease the names of Manco Capac's brothers allude to agricultural products that grow in different ecological areas, therefore representing the Inca domination of the lands for complementary agriculture, an element of certain success for the development of the Inca economy. The arrival of invaders and their conquest of a land certainly indicates a situation of domination established on a territory where different human groups lived together.

In other creation myths, in fact, the names of different ethnic groups appear as second names of Manco Capac's brothers, over which to first Inca dominated, evidently establishing a complex game of equilibrium with the so-called "Incas de Privilegio," who were the leaders of the non-Inca populations of the Cuzco area. The myth recounted by Juan de Betanzos, that of the four Ayar brothers, among whom was Manco Capac, apparently alludes to the same Ayarmaca people, with whom they had effectively established matrimonial alliances.

If, in fact, one looks beyond the myth, the little information available regarding early Inca history speaks of the various matrimonial alliances of the first three Inca rulers in the official list, namely Sinchi Roca, Lloque Yupanqui and Mayta Capac.

THE VERTICAL ARCHIPELAGOS

The cultural region of the Andes is, as we have seen, an area which in fact includes different geographical realities. These favored the development of different economic activities in the past and the present day. In the coastal areas, in the *yungas* and in inter-Andean valleys and part of the Amazon forest, it was possible to successfully cultivate many different agricultural products, while the highlands of the Cordillera were an almost inextinguishable source of the Andean camelids (mainly llamas and alpacas). Besides this, the Cordillera is extremely rich in minerals, with many different ones extracted from lava. Among these was obsidian, which was used for the blades of tools and knives. There are also natural salt deposits: not far from Cuzco, for example, the Maras reserves, which have been known and used from antiquity. These resources were concentrated in different ecological areas of the territory: soon Andean man learnt that access to these different areas was an extraordinary opportunity for a wider range of products. This led parts of the populace to establish themselves areas with different kinds of agricultural produce, occupying odd patches of territory according to a system that the great Andes expert John Murra called "vertical archipelagos" or "complementary verticality." Even the salt mines were frequented by people of different multiethnic communities of "colonizers," salt being a precious commodity that could mainly be obtained in the region's Andean area.

But how was this work organized? How were the products managed, considering that there were no markets in the area, nor money and not even, from a certain point of view, any levies as we consider them today? The mechanism of the Andean economy was based on the double track of reciprocity and the redistribution of strengths. In each Andean community, made up of different *ayllu* – i.e., extended families – people had the duty to give work to their family group, to carry out jobs for the common good. For example, this included the maintenance of fields and the herding of animals. Each relative therefore could count on help from his group. This bond between individuals also existed between individuals and nature: the maintenance of the land was necessary for it to give man its produce. Land was not seen as the property of man but as an almost divine natural element that should have been treated with respect; it was not "possessed" but managed by those who discharged their reciprocal duties to it.

Work which needed a higher form of organization, such as the construction and maintenance of an agricultural terrace, a road or a bridge, were not managed at an *ayllu* level but on the ethnic authority level of the so-called curaca, or landlords who organized the *mita*, the collective work shifts. This system still survives today and is fundamental for communities that still live according to traditional economies. In Tawantinsuyu the state administration organized the work shifts, which sometimes necessitated the transfer of people to work in areas with other labor groups, establishing ethnic enclaves far from the areas of origin. As one can imagine, these also represented presidia for control on particularly critical areas.

76 - The amazing rounded Terraces of Moray, in the Cuzco region, were the site of innovative agriculture during the Inca period.

77 - This image from Guaman Poma de Ayala's *Chronicle* (1613-15) depicts a group of at work on the plots that the Inca assigned to them.

TRAVAXO
ÇARA TARPVY MITAN

2

THE CONSTRUCTION OF THE STATE

THE CONSOLIDATION OF INCA POWER IN THE CUZCO VALLEY

Inca history, as written by its chroniclers, gives an official list of the sovereigns following the death of their founder-ancestor, Manco Capac. But the actual truth about the initial phases of the Cuzco history are still too shrouded in mystery for us to be able to pinpoint with certainty the events and people involved in them. There are various versions of the lives and events of the Inca lords in this period but, as often happens in the history of the Andean region, a series of typical names and titles are repeated for various people, which certainly does not aid clarity. In addition, the Spanish had a natural tendency to relate a linear type of history, with a dynastic succession of first-born sons in which sovereignty passed from father to son in a linear way. Instead, very often the younger sons were the ones to succeed to the throne after demonstrating great ability. This created much confusion for the chroniclers who had to describe the history of the country just conquered. What does appear to be certain is that the relations between the Incas and the local sovereigns were very close, so close, in fact, that many scholars believe that the Incas were subjugated to other groups – for example to the abovementioned Ayarmaca – during this phase and that they subsequently managed to achieve a sort of equal rank with them through a series of shrewd marriages. The son of Manco, Sinchi Roca, and his successors Lloque Yupanqui, Mayta Capac and Capac Yupanqui all carried out a policy which aimed to establish local equilibrium. According to María Rostworowski, the division of Cuzco into four parts is owed to the Ayarmaca, and this structure was to become the basis for the division of the empire. The archaeological data available for this period (even if it is not possible either to confirm or refute the names and facts given by the various chroniclers) tell us about a series of changes which took place in a generalized way throughout the whole Cuzco area. For example, we learn of the development of many sites and an increase in the production of ceramics and other luxury goods that testified to the greater importance of the area. Some local settlements, for example, Choquepuquio, were occupied discontinuously during various periods from the Huari era to the Inca imperial one without showing any traces of violent conquest or of fortifications reflecting a situation of conflict in the area. Nevertheless, Choquepuquio is in an area south of Cuzco, where other ethnic groups prevailed (the Pinagua, the Chilque and the Masque) and their names appear in some versions of the myths related to the first-born line of descent of the Incas. All thing considered, however, it is possible that the Incas did originally have good neighborly relations with some of these ethnic groups, especially with the small settlements south of Cuzco which probably accepted Inca patronage with good grace.

The Incas began to acquire power on the regional level during the reign of the sixth Inca, Inca Roca, who is considered to be the founder of the *hanan* Cuzco, or rather Upper Cuzco. Their increase in power was reflected in a reorganization of the capital of the future empire that was always to be the heart of the Inca world. María Rostworoski has recently brought to light some sources that give an ancient account of the division of the city into four quarters. However, the Inca Pachacutec's vigorous reorganization of the city layout after the earthquake of 1650 – and the subsequent one due to the Spanish conquest – are great obstacles to our acquiring a full understanding of the capital's earliest phases. The precise nature and extent of the initial settlement of Cuzco are not at all well known. We are not even sure that the city was called Cuzco. Some historians believe that this name was given to it only much later and that the village, located between the rivers Huatanay and Tullumayo, was originally called Acamama. This village had existed and had been frequented since the *Killke* period. Viracocha, the eighth Inca, began an expansionist policy toward the territories to the southeast and managed to prevail over some of the local groups (the Cana and the Canchi). After having gained a new prestigious position, the Incas were about to take part in the battles between the two most important kingdoms in the Titicaca area, the

Qolla and the Lupaqa. The Incas had decided to ally themselves with the Lupaqa, which had already won the war against the Qolla and established a pact of alliance with the people of Cuzco. The conquest of lands hundreds of miles from Cuzco was an important advance in the expansionist policy of the Children of the Sun. Scholars agree that this moment marked the beginning of the Incas' great expansion. Some historians, including Garcilaso de la Vega (1609), consider this expansion to have been a slow and almost peaceful civilizing movement outward from the center. Other authors, including Pedro Sarmiento de Gamboa (1572), believe that the Inca expansion was a violent and explosive one. The Garcilaso view of a noble native line was the most popular one, because his works had been translated into many languages and his view matched the idyllic and utopian idea of an empire based on justice and peace. This idealistic view had acquired a certain amount of popularity in the Western romantic literature. Today, almost all scholars agree that the expansion of the empire happened in an explosive way during a period of 50 to 100 years. This achievement appears astonishing and incredible if we think of it as reflecting the European model of military conquests. However, such thinking does not contribute to the understanding of the explosion of the Tawantinsuyu because today we know that in many areas the Incas simply made pacts of allegiance with the local lords, the *curacas*, who continued to govern their small communities without any violent change of power. In some cases, the Inca sovereigns married the daughters of the local chiefs to sanctify their new ties with the lands of their expansion. In this way, some of the most militarily active Inca sovereigns managed to find themselves married to even one hundred wives!

78 - *Queros* are ceremonial containers made of wood or precious metals. They have either geometrical or figurative decorations. This specimen has the shape of a human head (Museo Inca de la Universidad San Antonio Abad, Cuzco).

80-81 - This table depicts the busts of Inca rulers (Pedro de Osma Museum, Lima).

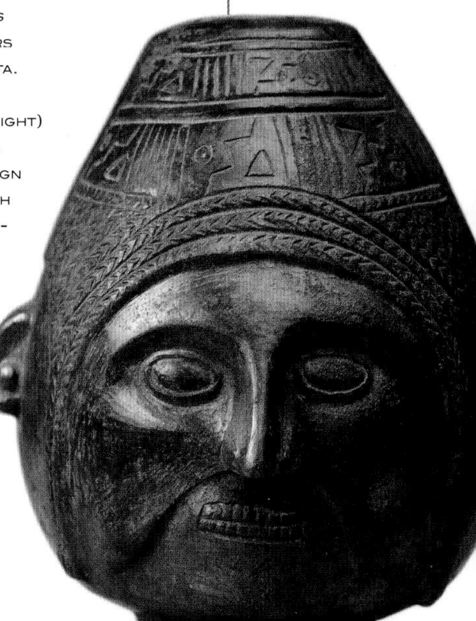

81 bottom - *Arybalos* are typical containers of made of terracotta. This specimen (9 inches/23 cm in height) depicts the head of a male figure. The design comes from the north coast of Peru (Chimú-Inca, 15th-16th centuries) (Museo Nacional de Arqueología, Antropología e Historia del Perú, Lima).

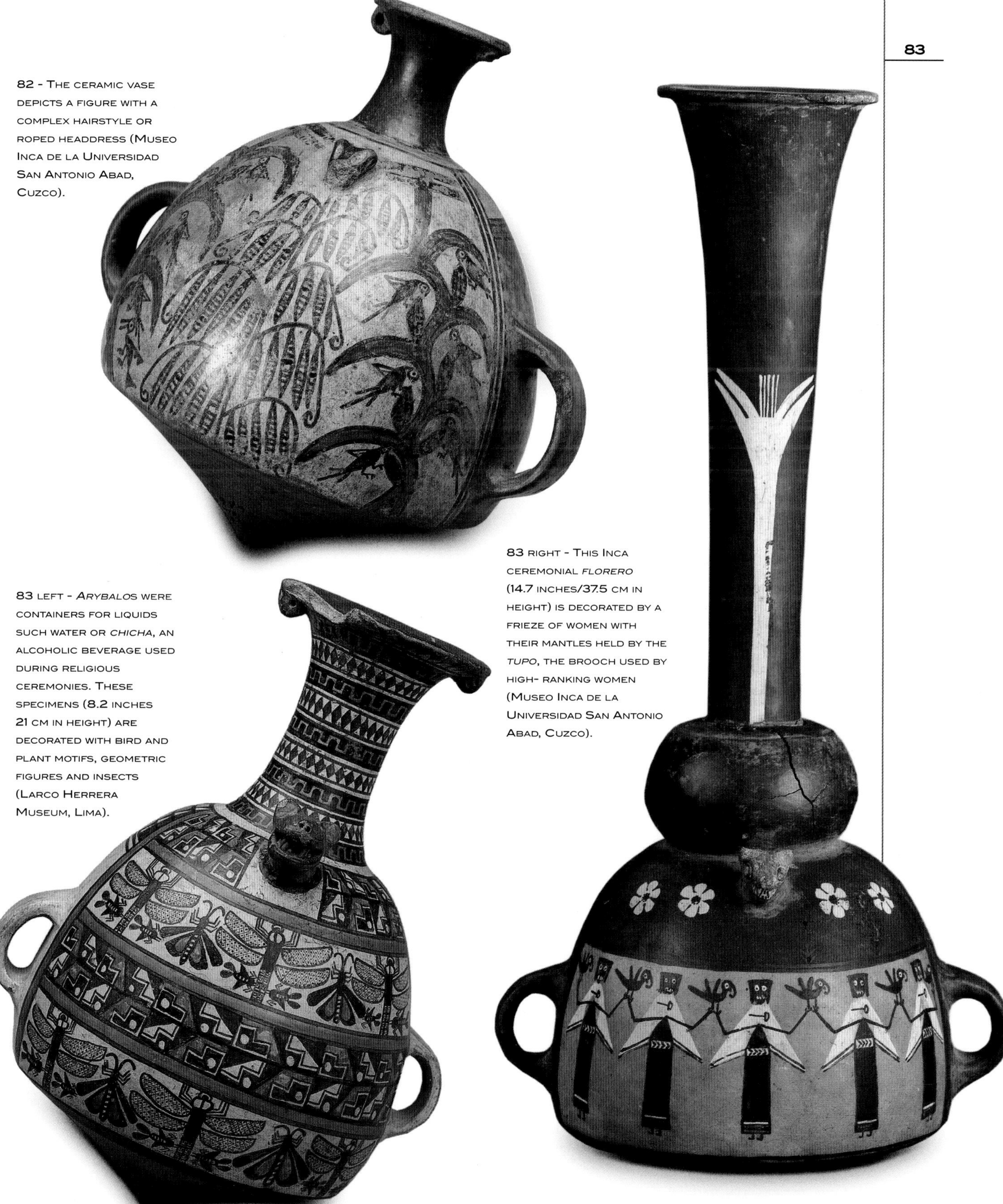

82 - The ceramic vase depicts a figure with a complex hairstyle or roped headdress (Museo Inca de la Universidad San Antonio Abad, Cuzco).

83 left - *Arybalos* were containers for liquids such water or *chicha*, an alcoholic beverage used during religious ceremonies. These specimens (8.2 inches 21 cm in height) are decorated with bird and plant motifs, geometric figures and insects (Larco Herrera Museum, Lima).

83 right - This Inca ceremonial *florero* (14.7 inches/37.5 cm in height) is decorated by a frieze of women with their mantles held by the *tupo*, the brooch used by high- ranking women (Museo Inca de la Universidad San Antonio Abad, Cuzco).

DIVINE SOVEREIGNS AND THE PRE-HISPANIC CUZCO NOBILITY

The first Inca, Manco Capac, son of the creator god Viracocha, had to endure a long period of vagrancy and many hardships before being able to establish himself in the promised land, in the Cuzco area. Even though the figure of Manco Capac has not been historically confirmed, it is clear that the Incas handed down this legend and saw it as a model for an Inca sovereign whose actions set the standards for exemplary behavior in all the sovereigns to come. This was true to such an extent that the most celebrated Inca, Pachacutec, is also called the "son of Manco Capac" because, he more than the others, incarnated the prototype of a sovereign of the Children of the Sun. This exemplary behavior emphasizes the role of the king as a tireless conqueror whose qualities of courage and bravery justify his status as the "chosen one." Even Pachacutec was a younger son who ascended to the throne through his courage. Some scholars have hypothesized that this was one of the reasons for the Inca's aggressive expansionist policy. Others, instead, believe that the military skills of the Incas were only relevant during their earliest period when they were starting to build their empire and that, subsequently, some of the conquests attributed to specific sovereigns were only inventions used to increase their warrior image. This is the case of the conquests of lands very near to the city of Cuzco made by the eleventh Inca, Huayna Capac because these lands had probably already been under imperial Inca domination for some time. This Inca sovereign used symbolic actions to reaffirm his power over the territory which had seen harsh battles during the mythological times of Manco Capac. The figure of the Inca as a political leader is emphasized in every way: both because of his decisive role in battle (in both positive and negative episodes) and because of the miraculous nature which often marked his participation in battle. It does seem to be certain that, in the final years of the empire, the Inca sovereign chose the son to succeed him when he was still alive. This was to avoid bloodshed and fierce battles for succession after his death. Some authors attribute this innovation to Pachacutec, who not only ordained his son as Inca when still alive but who also began the custom that the *coya*, or Inca's wife, was to be his sister in order to "dilute" the royal blood as little as possible. Once he ascended to power, the Inca represented the sun god on earth and became the highest military and religious leader of his people. His role did not end even after his death. In fact, the royal Inca mummies continued to have an active role in public and religious ceremonies. These mummies were dressed and fed exactly as they had been when they were alive and were proudly displayed in processions. Some scholars have hypothesized that the view of a father to son descent was Eurocentric and that it did not reflect the real political situation of the empire, especially in its early stages. One of the most careful Spanish chroniclers, Cieza de León (1553), had even described the reign as a diarchy where two sovereigns ruled together, one representing the *hanan* and the other the *hurin* half of Cuzco, or rather the upper and lower parts of the capital. The status of sovereign, which the Incas believed made the ruler all-powerful and a god on earth and who also had boundless wisdom and magnificent generosity, often clashed with the deeply human reality of the power games played by Cuzco's noble families. This was particularly true of the *panaqas*, who maneuvered to influence the politics and choices of the Incas. The *panaqas* were family groups founded in life by each Inca and comprised of his relatives. These groups had the duty to administer the sovereign's wealth and to perpetuate the cult of his mummy after his death. They carried these tasks out by considering the harvests of the royal lands as goods. Many Incas owned royal lands in the fertile Sagrado Valley (the agricultural area between Urubamba and Vilcanota to the north and south of Cuzco). There were ten *panaqas* in existence when the Spanish entered Cuzco. We do not know if that was their original number or if the *orejones* (or "big-eared men" as the Spanish called them because they wore large, heavy earrings which deformed the lobes of their ears as a mark of elite rank) had reorganized them or if the *panaqas* had been reorganized during particularly critical periods in the life of the empire.

84 - A person's rank was indicated by the richness of his headdress: this feather-decorated wool turban belonged to a high Inca dignitary (David Bernstein Collection, New York).

85 - The *uncu* was a kind of shirt used in the pre-Hispanic period. This wool specimen from the cemetery of Ancon belonged to a high dignitary (Ethnologisches Museum, Berlin).

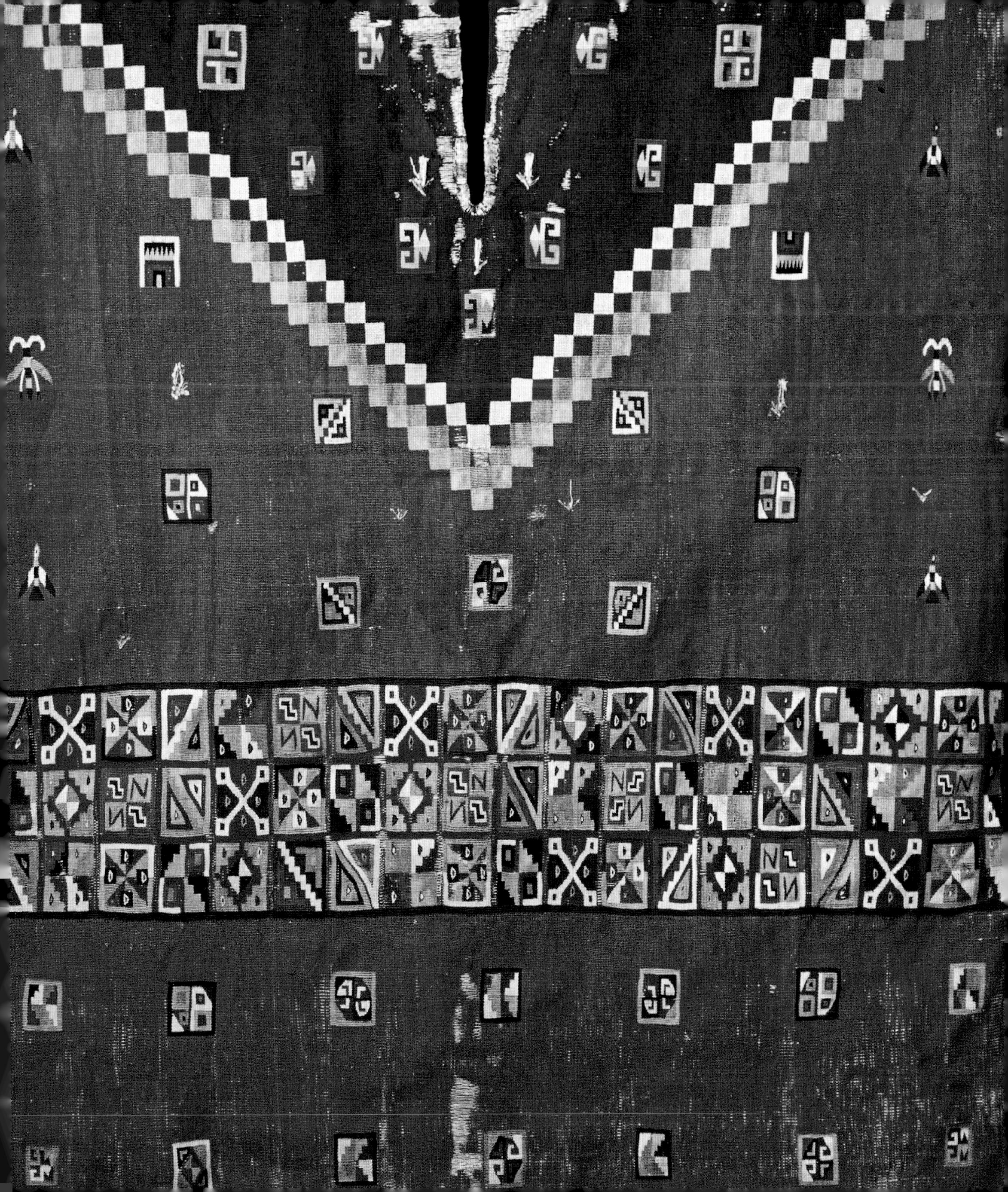

86 left - Figures could be depicted nude, as in this male gold statuette (8.9 inches/22.7 cm h) or wrapped in cloth, which is not always preserved (Dumbarton Oaks Collection, Washington, D.C.).

86 center left - Quite often Inca dignitaries, as in this golden statuette (6.4 inches/16.4 cm in height), are portrayed with cheeks swollen from chewing coca leaves. Coca was a medicinal plant used for the relief of weariness and for divination in the pre-Hispanic period (Museo de América, Madrid).

86 center right - The elongated ear lobes of the male figurines (8.9 inches/22.7 cm in height) resulted from wearing large, heavy earrings, a symbol of the elite that earned the Incas the definition of *orejones* (big ears) from the Spanish (Dumbarton Oaks Collection, Washington, D.C.).

86 right - In the Inca figurines, sexual attributes, in this case male, are emphasized. They should be understood in terms of the propitious qualities, particularly fertility, that these statues encompassed (Museo de América, Madrid).

87 - This silver statuette with encrustations in gold, stone and shell, depicts a man in the typical Inca standing position with hands crossed on the chest (Ethnologisches Museum, Berlin).

CVSCO.

CUZCO, THE CAPITAL OF THE EMPIRE

For the Incas, the construction of Cuzco meant much more than just planning an area to live in: it was the construction of a holy city and the navel of the world from which everything spread outward. The lines dividing the territory into four *suyu*, or parts, began from the center of the Coricancha, the golden enclosure and the most sacred place of all where the sun god and his earthly incarnation, the Inca, were celebrated. The Incas called their territory Tawantinsuyu, which included "all Four Parts Together." These parts were Chinchaysuyu (the lands to the northwest), Antisuyu (those to the northeast), Kollasuyu (the vast lands to the south which extended to Chile and Argentina) and the coastal area of Cuntisuyu (to the west).

The city, too, was divided into parts: an upper one (*hanan*) and a lower one (*hurin*). This division corresponded to the division of the empire into four parts and, in fact, the *hanan* parts were Antisuyu and Chinchaysuyu while the *hurin* parts were Cuntisuyu and Kollasuyu.

The division between upper and lower was political, not only topographical. The most important families lived in the upper part, at least beginning from a certain period. They were often in conflict for power with the equally high-ranking – but not as powerful – families of *hurin* Cuzco. Tom Zuidema, the celebrated scholar of Andean history, has successfully supported the hypothesis that the same type of division is present in many Andean civilizations, not only in that of the Incas. This division is linked to a certain psychological Andean quality according to which "lower" is associated with time past and the "before." It is not coincidental that the most ancient families of Cuzco lived in *hurin* Cuzco, while the families which were part of the governing elite – starting from the ascent to power by Pachacutec (the sovereign responsible for the reorganization of many imperial institutions) lived in *hanan* Cuzco.

Linked to the *suyu* and to the division of the empire (whose dividing lines began from the the Coricancha, the symbolic center of the city) were the *ceques*, or rather the imaginary lines which united various sacred sites in the territory surrounding the city and linked them to its center. The maintenance of the sacred places was entrusted to extended families (*ayllu*) and to the *panaqas* according to well-defined apportionment and was performed at specific times of the years. These events also regulated the agricultural calendar. The *ceques* system may well be the most illuminating example of how the Incas linked the territory to their concept of the sacred and how the maintenance of these sacred sites was not only an economic activity but was also pervaded by profound religiosity. Since the *ceques* followed the general division of Cuzco and of the empire into four parts, those who participated in the rituals through their participation felt themselves to be an integrating part of a much broader system beyond the whole four-part empire.

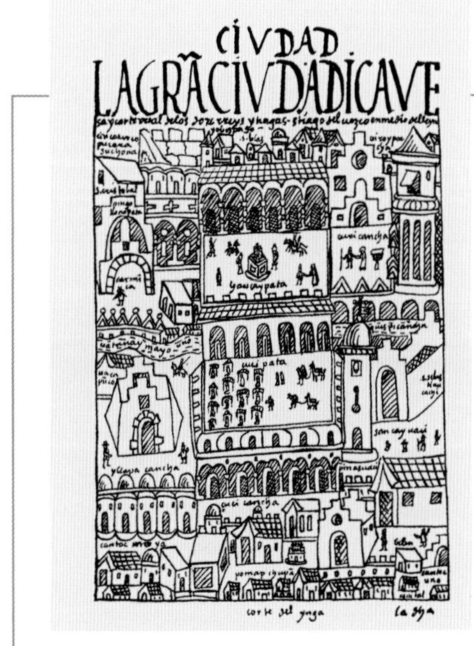

88 - This drawing from Georgius Braun's *Civitates Orbis Terrarum* (1572) shows the orthogonal plan of Cuzco's center, a legacy of the Huari tradition. The detail depicts an Inca being carried in a litter.

89 - This drawing from Guaman Poma de Ayala's *Chronicle* illustrates Cuzco's main square. The drawing shows the route of the river which flowed through the city and the systematic placement of some older buildings.

90 - In this clay model of an Inca residential section and its enclosure one notes the placement of the buildings which open on the *cancha*, the central open space typical of Inca settlements (Museo Inca de la Universidad Nacional San Antonio Abad, Cuzco).

91 - The terracotta building model (7.9 inches/20.2 cm in height) is from the Inca era and comes from the northern coast of Peru (Chimú-Inca culture, 15th-16th centuries). One notes the double thatched roof typical of the buildings of the Sierra (Museo de América, Madrid).

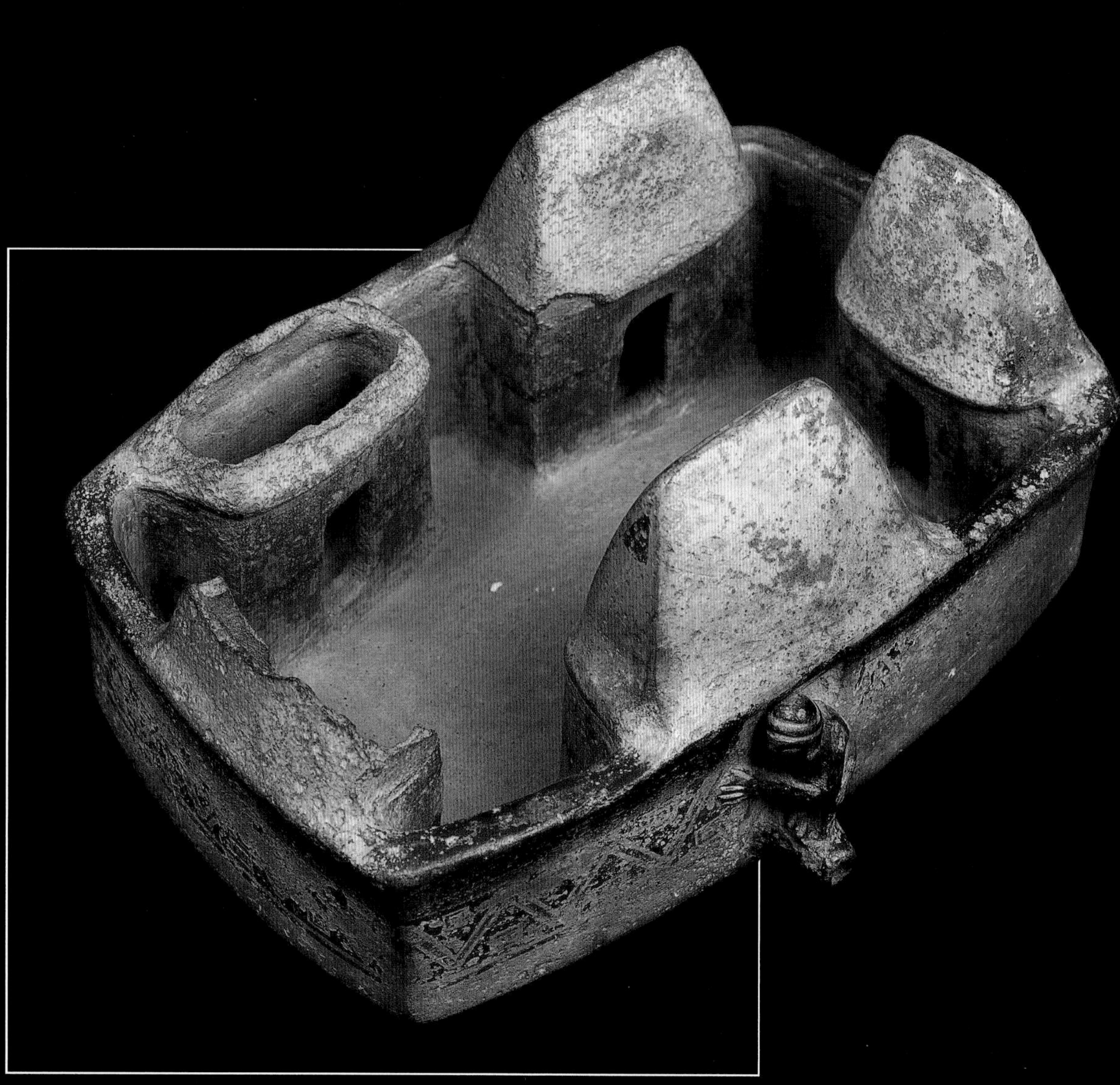

A vast network of roads united the territory's sacred sites but also had the very worldly purposes of ensuring connections to the provinces, permitting the movement of armies and the reception of the goods which flowed into Cuzco as a mark of the capital's ties with the lands and with the ethnic groups that the Royal Trail, or Capac Ñan, had traversed.

Totaling 14,300 miles (23,000 km) in length in winding its way through Argentina, Bolivia, Chile, Colombia Ecuador and Peru, the Inca road system was the most important infrastructure to have been built in the Americas prior to the Spanish conquest. This road system, the Capac Ñan, had two main highways: one in the *sierra* part and the other along the coast, and these were united by many cross-roads. The Inca road system strongly impressed the Spanish because of its precise construction and efficient maintenance but also because, besides its roads, it included suspended rope bridges, steep stairways carved into rock and postal stations or *tambos*, which were arranged at regular intervals along the path. Some roads on the coast were even protected from the desert sand by shielding them with walls made of sun-baked bricks (what we call adobe).

The most important segment of the Capac Ñan was the one running along the Andean ridge that connected Cuzco to what were to become the main imperial cities at the height of the empire's splendor – and these cities obviously were located in proximity to the Capac Ñan. In some areas of the Peruvian territory, Inca penetration was not particularly important and was limited solely to the area crossed by the Capac Ñan. This, for example, is the case of the Inca site of Huaritambo, in the Conchucos area, which was built on the Capac Ñan probably by local workers and used as a postal station and as a warehouse for the storage of food supplies and wool of the llamas of this fertile area.

Today, thanks to an important project promoted by Peru's National Institute of Culture for the mapping of the entire Capac Ñan for its inclusion in the UNESCO list of Human Heritage Sites, we finally know a great deal more about this important in-

frastructure. For example, we now know that the Incas, besides building many of the Capac Ñan segments from scratch, also restored road systems which the ocal populations had used for more than 2000 years and that the Incas finished building the road branches connecting the various ethnic groups by imposing work shifts, or *mita*, on the local populations. In addition, we are only beginning to learn about the wealth of building techniques, materials and strategic arrangements that went into this astonishing road system.

92 - Wiñay Wayna, in Urubamba Valley, forms part of the network of royal properties in the Machu Picchu archaeological park. The city is located on an extremely steep and completely terraced hill.

92-93 - At Wiñay Wayna terracing for agricultural purposes was used but ceremonial structures were also present in the settlement, such as the one in this image. There were also residences which welcomed noble Inca families, who periodically stayed in them.

93 bottom - Phuyupatamarca is an Inca city situated in the Urubamba region, not far from Machu Picchu. The building formed part of the network of royal properties united by Capac Ñan, located in the direction of the forest.

THE PRINCIPLES OF THE INCA RELIGION

There is no concept of a single creator god in the Andean religion; rather there is that of a vital breath called *camac* in the Quechua language. This vital breath is innate in some divinities which, in the creation myths, contribute to populating the world in different ways according to the culture examined. In addition, the peoples of the Andes shared another important principle: the *pacarina* or place of origin of a people but also of plants and animals which were normally in a specific area of the territory (a lagoon, a grotto or a mountain). The *pacarina* were very important sites that were sacred and dangerous at the same time because they were the places where man could communicate with the sacred entities. The contemporary rural populations of the Andes often venerated and feared these sites and frequented them only after carrying out the required ritual practices. As we have seen, the chroniclers have described various *pacarinas* including Lake Titicaca, the city of Tiwanaku and the grotto of Pacaritambo.

The Incas called the temples and objects considered to be sacred *huacas*. Even images of the divinities were considered to be *huacas* because they are believed to be animated by the divine principle. In addition, specific natural shapes – possibly, a split in a rock or a strangely shaped ear of corn – were also considered to be *huacas*.

In addition to the sacredness associated with natural elements in the territory, there was also an official and formal religion which included a number of divinities, though the most important god of the Incas was the sun god or Inti.

A statue of the sun god stood in the Coricancha temple (in its golden center), in the heart of the capital. The Incas believed that the moon, Quilla, was the wife of the sun and she too was venerated as a divinity. The sun and the moon, considered to be respectively the male and female forces, were opposed and complementary at the same time. These forces well represent the sense of Andean dualism and they had their earthly incarnation in the figure of the Inca and his *coya*, bride/sister. The royal couple, as in the beginning of the Inca story about Manco Capac and Mama Ocllo, represented the unity and equilibrium of the opposing forces in the world; these are in constant and necessary opposition: right and left, high and low, man and woman, etc. The two halves of the world (which could be seen as multiplying in an infinite number of forms in a complex play of mirrors) were often called upon, particularly in Inca art, through the use of two metals: gold (believed to be the sweat of the sun) and silver (believed to be the tears of the moon).

94 LEFT - THE CEREMONIAL STRUCTURES OF THE ISLAND OF THE SUN IN LAKE TITICACA (BOLIVIA) PROVIDE EVIDENCE OF THE INCAS' DESIRE TO BIND THEIR OWN RELIGIOUS TRADITION TO THAT OF THE IMPORTANT LAKE TITICACA REGION, WHICH THEY CONSIDERED A *PACARINA* OR SACRED PLACE OF ORIGIN.

94 RIGHT - THE MAIN TEMPLE DEDICATED TO VIRACOCHA IN THE CITY OF RAQCHI IN THE CUZCO REGION, EXTENDS FOR 301 FT (92 M) ON A HEIGHT OF 75 FT TO FORM AN ENORMOUS STRUCTURE WITH A STONE AND ADOBE BASE, OF WHICH JUST A SMALL SECTION REMAINS INTACT.

95 - THE FEAST FOR INTI, OR THE SUN GOD, WAS CELEBRATED IN DECEMBER, PRESIDED OVER BY THE INCA, WHO WAS CONSIDERED THE SON OF THE SUN GOD (FROM GUAMAN POMA DE AYALA'S *CHRONICLE*, 1613-15).

DEZIEMBRE
CAPAC INTI RAIMI
la gran pascua solene del sol
capac

96 - In this cat-shaped *quero* the circular decorations symbolize the animal's spots. A hunting scene is depicted on the walls (Museo Inca de la Universidad Nacional San Antonio Abad, Cuzco).

97 LEFT - ON MANY *QUEROS* GEOMETRIC SCROLLS OR *TOCAPU* WERE REPRESENTED. THESE HAD A FUNCTION SIMILAR TO THAT OF WESTERN HERALDIC SYMBOLS (MUSEO INCA DE LA UNIVERSIDAD NACIONAL SAN ANTONIO ABAD, CUZCO).

97 RIGHT - THIS *QUERO*, DECORATED WITH A FRIEZE OF FEMALE FIGURES IN THE CENTRAL BAND, BELONGS TO THE INCA CULTURE AND COMES FROM THE LAKE TITICACA REGION (MUSEO NACIONAL DE ARQUEOLOGÍA, LA PAZ, BOLIVIA).

98 - The votive Inca figurines were extremely stereotyped: female figures were always depicted with long hair falling on their back (Museo Inca de la Universidad Nacional San Antonio Abad, Cuzco).

99 - Inca figurines are often paired to represent the Andean duality, one of the most important concepts of the pre-Hispanic cosmovision (Museo Inca de la Universidad Nacional San Antonio Abad, Cuzco).

100-101 - The funerary rituals of high-ranking persons occupied a predominant place in the pre-Hispanic society. In this extraordinary depiction a number of figures (in wood or shell) accompany the *fardo* or funerary blanket during a procession (Chimú culture, 11th-14th centuries) (Maahun, Trujillo)

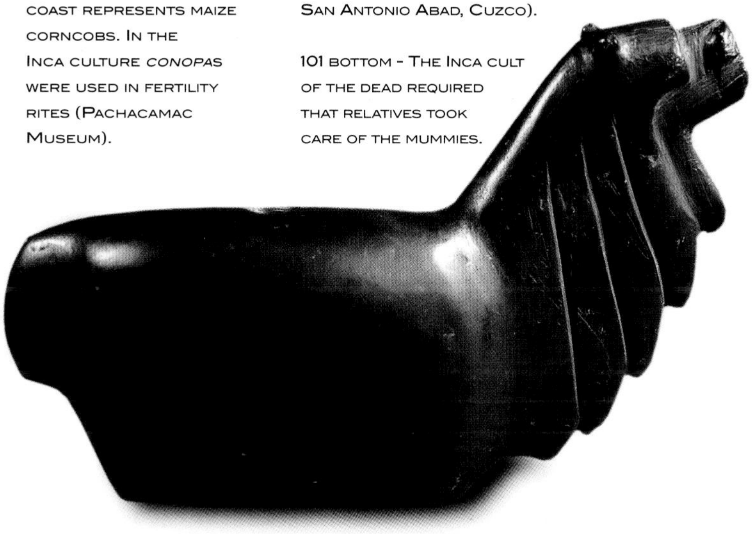

101 top - This stone *conopa* (1.3 inches/3.5 cm in height) from the Pachacamac temple on Peru's central coast represents maize corncobs. In the Inca culture *conopas* were used in fertility rites (Pachacamac Museum).

101 center - The stone statues (*illas*) of llamas assured the fertility of the flocks (Museo Inca de la Universidad Nacional San Antonio Abad, Cuzco).

101 bottom - The Inca cult of the dead required that relatives took care of the mummies.

The Incas also paid homage to other divinities and brought the effigies of the *huacas* of the peoples they conquered to Cuzco to take their place alongside the Inca ones in the Coricancha. Particular attention was accorded to the *huacas* that were considered to be oracles. These oracles were functioning at the time of the Inca expansion in the territory of Peru and they included the very powerful one of Pachacamac, located a few miles south of Lima. These sites, even though they did not specifically belong to the Cuzcan religion, were considered to be so important that Inca presence was an indispensable mark of political power.

Sacred objects included the mummies of the founding ancestors of the ethnic groups. The Incas took great pains to preserve the bodies of certain important people because they believed that their mummies had the power to intercede for them with the afterlife. Tombs were periodically re-opened to bring gifts to these mummies and to gain their participation in the lives of the living, as we are told in various chronicles of the native world. Naturally, a cult of the dead, in relation to family and clan, also existed.

Lastly, there were fertility cults dedicated to Mother Earth, or *pachamama*, and cults on the family level to ensure fertile fields and thriving flocks. One custom consisted of burying small images portraying animals or plants in the ground; these images were called *illas* and *conopas*.

3

THE EXPANSIONIST POLICY

THE INCA PACHACUTEC AND THE WAR AGAINST THE CHANCA

In the 1440s a sovereign came to power who changed the destiny of the Tawantinsuyu: Pachacutec Inca Yupanqui, whose name not by chance means "he who revolutionizes the earth." The 16-century chroniclers attributed several innovations to this revolutionizer and also the foundation of some institutions that were to become the strong points of the empire; they tend to consider him a figure comparable to that of Manco Capac, the mythical founder of the Inca people. Even the story of this sovereign is marked by a divine pre-destination which manifested itself at the moment when the young man first entered battle, in the so-called war against the Chanca, a group of invaders coming from the Andahuaylas area. While the Manco legend bears witness, in the Andean manner, to the establishment of the Inca in the Cuzco area, the mythical war against the Chanca is the narrative transposition of another key moment in Inca history, namely, the beginning of their expansion.

It is noteworthy that in the Inca oral tradition, the first expansionistic phase of Pachacutec's policy tells of a period in which the Inca ruler was forced to dedicate himself to the conquest of the territories in the regional arc around Cuzco (in this case by means of the Chanca war), which his predecessors had gained. As we will see, each Inca was to have the same problem: to reaffirm his power on the lands of Manco Capac's conquest. Some researchers thought that this was necessary because each sovereign, in the first phase of his reign, had to reaffirm symbolically (perhaps even materially) his position with the (then) subjugated "Incas de privilegio" to show his warrior qualities in the same way which Manco Capac did at the beginning of the story.

The great battle against the Chanca is difficult to set in time: the source which best tells it is the chronicle of Juan de Betanzos, who probably learned of it from his wife, the noble Cusirimay Oello, from the Pachacutec *panaca*. It is clear then that this Spanish chronicle is embedded with a positive and epic vision of the life of Pachacutec, who was crowned as the chosen one to lead the Incas to the conquest of the whole Andean territory. According to María Rostworowski, the Chanca had in truth been competing with the Inca for quite some time, perhaps since the era of the reign of Viracocha.

The Chanca said, like the Inca, that they had emerged from a lagoon (Choclococha), and were organized in two confederate groups (*hanan* and *hurin*), which dated back to their mythical founder ancestors (one from the *hanan* half, the other from the *hurin* half of the human group). By undertaking an aggressive expansion policy, perhaps using the occasional alliances with other groups such as the Huancas, the Chanca came to clash with the Inca: the myth narrates of them having sent a war message to the Inca Viracocha who,

103 - This pendant with holes (it was probably sewn onto fabric) is made of a gold disc (4.3 inches/11 cm in diameter) to which is fastened a mobile figure. The mask indicates that the object is from the Sicán-Lambayeque culture (Bruning Museum, Lambayeque).

not confident that he could beat them, took refuge in a fortress outside Cuzco with his two sons. The epic tale that Betanzos recounts is not devoid of details or episodes of a distinctive European flavor and in particular tells how the menace revealed itself to be a positive episode for the Children of the Sun. The cadet son of Viracocha, Pachacutec, the only one who wished to challenge the invaders, was visited in a dream by the god Viracocha who predicted that he would be victorious if he entered battle against the Chanca.

On the day of the battle Pachacutec could only count on his own strength, seeing that no-one else was supporting him. However, in a critical moment of the conflict a miracle took place: some stones (later called the *pururaucas*) magically turned into ferocious warriors who dissipated the enemy, terrified by the prodigy. As many researchers have rightly observed, this story sounds more like a European medieval epic tale than a prodigious event in line with the Andean tradition, especially with regard to the apparition of the god Viracocha in a dream. In fact, the "manner" in which the more reliable indigenous sources refer to interaction with the sacred (for example, to interrogate divinities on the future), is through oracles and after numerous and complex sacrifices. Only with difficulty do the divinities appear in dreams to predict directly the future. This is just one of the objections that lead one to doubt the truth of Betanzos' account. There are in fact two sources that deny that the war took place under Pachacutec, but rather that it occurred much earlier. Others omit this event completely. For some researchers, such as Pierre Duviols, the episode was completely invented to glorify the figure of Pachacutec and to justify his voracious conquest of the Andean territory that marked his reign.

Undoubtedly, the battle against the Chanca was a watershed: with these heroic deeds, eliminating the competition from the brother who had been destined to rise to the Inca throne and defeating the resistance of his father, Pachacutec obtained the *mazcaypaycha*, the red bow which designated the power of the Inca soveregin. The conquest was so important and significant that chronicler Polo de Ondegardo (who found the mummy of Pachacutec, many years after his death in a temple dedicated to Thunder in Tococache) says that he rested near the idol of the Chanca. It was an Inca custom to take possession of the idols and the mummies of the ancestors of defeated enemy groups, as this was equivalent to reaffirming the victory and achieving dominance over them for once and all.

Once he obtained power and possession of significant booty, Pachacutec began to construct a fit capital and to expand his aims beyond the regional confines.

104 - This drawing by Guaman Poma de Ayala depicts the Inca ruler Pachacutec as a conquering warrior.

105 - The Incas fight against a local ethnic group (from Guaman Poma de Ayala's *Chronicle*).

PACHACUTEC AND THE RE-ORGANIZATION OF CUZCO

Traditionally historians attribute to Pachacutec the re-ordering and expansion of the city of Cuzco, a process that lasted twenty long years. He is also to have built many of the structures that rightly made it famous. When we speaking of Cuzco it is necessary to emphasize that the current definition of city is misleading: Cuzco was essentially a sacred space in which a minimal part of the population resided, representing the political and religious elite of the empire. The remaining population lived just outside this symbolic center of the Inca world, and only entered in certain circumstances.

Cuzco is situated at 11,480 ft (3500 m) above sea level in the area between the rivers Huatanay and Tullumayo. Major transformations in the city's layout began right at the start of the colonial period to make space for the Spanish rulers' headquarters and for Catholic churches, reflecting the model of European cities of the time. These changes allow us to appreciate only partially the layout of Cuzco in Pachacutec's day. According to some researchers the whole urban space was organized to celebrate rituals and exalt the area's most important resource: its numerous natural water sources. In actuality, Cuzco was not a particularly easy place to defend, nor was it very well situated for communication and trade routes. It was simply an area where stone and water – the basic elements of the Andean region – were abundant.

The chronicles say that Pachacutec wanted to remodel the city, giving it the shape of a puma, whose head was the monumental complex of Sacsahuaman, which rises on the hill north of the city and whose construction was also begun by Pachacutec (but, as we have previously seen, the area was already frequented during the *Killke* period).

As it was also associated with the power of the Inca and the *kai pacha*, the "world on this side," the puma was an animal that Pachacutec particularly loved: according to chronicler Betanzos,

that Pachacutec presented himself as a re-founder of the Inca empire: celebrating the figure of Manco Capac was evidently a priority political operation as it represented power. The Temple, whose curved foundation wall still stands today and on which the Santo Domingo monastery was built, was the place where the statue of the Sun – in the form of the golden idol known as Punchao – was kept. It was also where the Temple of the Moon, Quilla ("wife" of the Sun) and the Temple of Thunder were located. Outside the complex was a sacred garden with reproductions of plants in gold and silver; they were symbolically planted every year during the planting and harvest seasons. Even in this case, with Cuzco being a holy place and the *imago mundi* of the Inca, a symbolic planting and harvest would take place here of reproductions made from sacred metals: gold representing the sun, silver the moon. This was to be the perfect prototype of all planting and harvesting in the fields of the empire.

The destruction of the Temple came almost immediately after the conquest, both because it naturally represented the indigenous population's most holy site and also because it was partly covered in gold slates which the Spanish removed and melted down. The same fate awaited many of the holy images kept in Cuzco. The gold, melted sown and cast into ingots, was more easily transported and was also easier to share among Pizarro's *conquistadores*, who claimed it as war plunder. In contrast, the gold and silver plants of the Coricancha garden were an inventory in images of the treasures given to Charles V as a testimony of the richness of the lands conquered in the New World.

the sovereign often paid homage to the most majestic feline in the Andes by masquerading with its coat on his back during the most solemn occasions.

Today, however, not all researchers agree that Cuzco reflects a puma shape; some identify a central nucleus from which the city's buildings radiate outward for 125 acres (50 hectares), together with another 250 acres (100 hectares) in the external belt, home to a population of about 150,000 people.

Pachacutec's restructuring resulted in some of the city's most important features: the Temple of the Sun (the Coricancha), "the golden rectangle," and the Sacsahuaman complex, respectively the back part of the puma's body and its head.

According to legend, the Sun Temple was built around what was perhaps the first area of Manco Capac's settlement in Cuzco – and it was not by chance that he chose a site where there were structures from the *Killke* period. We have noted

106-107 - After the Spanish conquest the Church of Santo Domingo was built on top of Cuzco's Temple of the Sun (the Coricacha). The ancient tightly interlocking stone-block walls are however still visible in the remains of the Inca building.

107 top - The most characteristic feature of Inca structures is the perfect fit of the stones without use of mortar, as can be noted in this detail of a wall of the palace of Sinchi Roca at Cuzco.

107 center - In Cuzco's Calle Loreto, one can still see parts of the walls of Inca palaces; they now form the bases of Spanish colonial structures.

107 bottom - Tambo Machay is located in the Cuzco region. It was an Inca sacred site and has a stream, close to which, as often was the case, a small temple was built.

The other imposing architectural project begun during Pachacutec's rule was construction of the Sacsahuaman complex. The grandiose structures are the result of a commitment that involved the population of the whole Cuzco valley. They worked to fulfill their reciprocal duties toward the Inca through their obligatory shift work, the *mita*. Some researchers hold that this great enterprise was possible because Pachacutec offered the local rulers conspicuous gifts

from the Chanca war loot: the rulers thanked him with the work of their peoples. What appears certain is that the magnificent undertaking of creating this enormous stone complex situated in the northern part of the city was begun by Pachacutec and was continued by his successors. According to chronicler Cieza de Léon, the construction involved 20,000 men. The magnificence of the work so impressed the Spanish that they described it as a citadel with buildings of different kinds: temples, houses, and towers with many riches hoarded therein. What now strikes visitors is the imposing nature of the stone blocks used for the three zigzag walls around the enormous site. These blocks, arranged to form in three overlapping terraces over 60 ft (18 m) high, are individually sometimes as much as 26 ft (8 m) in height. Pedro Sancho de la Hoz (one of Pizarro's captains and one of the first chroniclers of the history of Peru) wrote in 1534 that "No-one would every think that humans put them there"; an indication of just how huge they were. They were also perfectly squared and fitted together without any mortar, in the purest Inca imperial style. But one also notes walls of a different type; they probably date to the earliest phases of construction as they were built using different techniques. The terrace levels, also known as *baluartes* (bulwarks), were aligned on a north-south axis and have various apertures that acted as passageways.

But what was Sacsahuaman? Because of its imposing form and location at the top of a hill, it was traditionally identified it as a sort of fortress. But the presence of many holy structures, sculptures in the landscape, such as the famous "Inca Throne" (a natural rock sculpted into an object of worship like many other *huacas* of the same kind in the Cuzco area, including the famous Qenqo stone) have led scholars to believe that its defensive function was not incompatible with that of a temple complex where the whole population could gather for the Inca's "sponsored festivities," marking important moments in the religious calendar. In fact, the site has an ample esplanade where aqueducts, stone cisterns and many sculpted rocks compose a ritual area in which water plays a fundamental role. To this day, on the occasion of the June solstice a great revival festival takes place in Sacsahuaman (it celebrates the bond of the current population with its Inca past), whose main element is the ceremony known as Inti Raymi, the pre-Hispanic celebration of the sun god (Inti), which in the Inca period occurred during the solstice.

108-109 - The foundations of the so-called Muyuqmarka Tower in Sacsahuaman, the starting point for the channel system that drained water from the structure.

108 bottom and 109 top - Though believed to be a fortress on the basis of Spanish accounts, however, various buildings are found in Sacsahuaman, including houses, towers, warehouses, and ceremonial structures.

109 bottom - Sacsahuaman is a public and ceremonial complex which rises on a natural hill above Cuzco.

110-111 - In Sacsahuaman's *baluartes*, the stones, organized in three overlapping terraces which exceed 59 ft (18 m) in the height, some individual blocks measure 26.2 ft (8 m) in height.

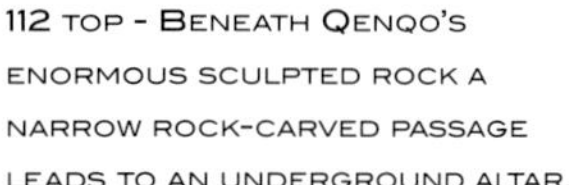

112 TOP - BENEATH QENQO'S ENORMOUS SCULPTED ROCK A NARROW ROCK-CARVED PASSAGE LEADS TO AN UNDERGROUND ALTAR.

112 CENTER - QENQO IS ONE THE SACRED COMPLEXES WHICH RISE ABOVE THE CITY OF CUZCO, NOT FAR AWAY FROM SACSAHUAMAN. IN FACT, QENQO IS A NATURAL ROCK OUTCROP THAT HAS BEEN ENTIRELY CUT INTO AND CARVED BY THE INCAS.

112 BOTTOM - QENQO'S ROCK MATRIX HAD BEEN SHAPED INTO STAIRS, ZIGZAGS AND OTHER FORMS SO THAT STREAMS FLOW IN THE INTERIOR, GIVING THE IMPRESSION OF AN ENORMOUS WATER-GAMES COMPLEX.

112-113 - FOR THE INCAS, A PARTICULAR ROCK OUTCROP, AS WELL AS MANY OTHER NATURAL ELEMENTS, COULD BE SACRED. IT IS THEREFORE COMMON TO FIND TEMPLE STRUCTURES BUILT CLOSE TO A REGION'S SIGNIFICANT NATURAL FEATURES, AS IS THE CASE WITH QENQO'S ENORMOUS ROCKY MASS.

PACHACUTEC'S ROYAL POSSESSIONS

In the Inca territorial administration system the Sun, as the supreme Inca divinity, had to possess some plots of land in each corner of the empire. The "high priest" of the Sun worship ritual, an official who was often a relative of the Inca, was responsible for the central administration of these lands, while the actual cultivation of them was undertaken by the local population as part of the work tribute owed to the Tawantinsuyu. As an *intipchurin* (a direct descendent of the Sun god), the Inca also had to own some land. We know that from the time of Pachacutec onward the Inca sovereigns accumulated possessions not only in the form of land, but also mineral sources, salt mines and settlements. Notwithstanding numerous royal holdings throughout the empire, the most elegant and famous were all in the Cuzco area, in the fertile and sunny Urubamba Valley. The sovereigns would visit these places where many servants lived, herding livestock, working in the fields, and producing goods. Upon the death of an Inca ruler, his possessions descended to his *panaca*.

To give an idea of how important these royal estates were, we have only to realize that Pachacutec's son, Topa Inca Yupanqui, owned whole villages (including Chinchero, now a popular tourist village where the foundations of an Inca building still stand) in addition to numerous other villages, some as far distant as the Titicaca area. Each of these villages had a population of about 4000 families. Pachacutec, too, had vast lands in the Urubamba Valley area which had come to him as a result of his political negotiations and his military conquests. In this area, north of Cuzco Pachacutec founded three of the most interesting settlements in the Inca world: Machu Picchu (which is one of numerous settlements of the same type in the northwestern part of Cuzco), Ollantaytambo and Pisac.

Pisac is a collection of extraordinary buildings, farmed terraces and temples set on a promontory in the Urubamba Valley. The group of buildings is on top of a mountain and Pisac's farmed terraces cascade beneath them for hundreds of feet until they reach the plain next the river.

114 - PISAC IS AN IMPERIAL ERA CITY, AS EVIDENCED BY THE PERFECTLY SQUARED STONES OF THE MAJOR BUILDINGS OF THE ELITE AND THE RELIGIOUS STRUCTURES, SHOWN IN THESE IMAGES.

115 - PISAC IS LOCATED IN THE FERTILE SAGRADO VALLEY AND OCCUPIES AN ENTIRE PROMONTORY WITH VARIOUS SECTORS SEPARATED BY DITCHES. THE VALLEY AND THE LOWER FLANKS OF THE MOUNTAIN ARE ENTIRELY TERRACED.

116-117 - The Intihuatana structures in Pisac are located around the main temple, which is built around an enormous natural rock outcrop.

117 - Slightly trapezoidal-shaped niches were built inside the structures and were used to place specific objects or for decorative purposes. The large ones could serve as look-out points for the building's sentries.

118-119 - The ruins of Pisac, located in the fertile Urubamba Valley, are famous for the incredible fusion between structures and landscape that Incas were able to produce.

Ollantaytambo presents a more compact picture. It is located about 25 miles (40 km) farther north on the same river. The modern city has covered part of the pre-Hispanic ruins but some canals and wall foundations are still visible near the main square. The best preserved part of the site is the so-called "Fortaleza" (fortress), an ensemble of structures which includes a remarkable Temple of the Sun, perched on a promontory whose access is defended by a very steep terraced climb. The construction of the Temple of the Sun has been the subject of lively debate among experts because the pink stone used to build its main wall is not found locally. In addition, on the same wall we find the iconographic Andean cross, which is a typical symbol in the ceremonial center of Tiwanaku in Bolivia. This can be explained by the fact that the Incas probably got their labor force from the locals of the Lake Titicaca area and these are famous for their masterful stone sculpture. It is believed that their skills were absorbed and re-elaborated by the Children of the Sun.

In Ollantaytambo, as on many royal estates in the Urubamba Valley, the abundant water was used not only for agricultural purposes but also to create a series of waterfalls that were pervaded by deep religious significance. Water, a vital element and considered by the Incas to be a pure divine emanation, was always present in sacred architecture. The springs were considered to be *huacas* and special receptacles, called *paccha* in the Quechua language, were used for the ritual sprinkling of liquids which reproduced the water courses similar to those of the Inca sacred aqueducts. It was specifically due to the abundance of water that the Inca managed to survive the siege of Ollantaytambo by the Spanish; they used this great resource to flood the plain below the Fortaleza, and thus put to flight the Spanish army led by Pizarro.

120 TOP - OLLANTAYTAMBO'S TEMPLE OF THE SUN IS BUILT WITH ROSY-COLORED ROCKS. THE PROTUBERANCES WERE PERHAPS DECORATIVE ELEMENTS OR FOOTHOLDS USED TO HELP BUILDERS TO MOVE AND POSITION THE BLOCKS.

120 BOTTOM - THE BEST PRESERVED PART OF THE CITY IS THE SO-CALLED FORTRESS.

120-121 - OLLANTAYTAMBO RISES ON VARIOUS PEAKS, JOINED AT THE VALLEY BOTTOM BY THE TERRACING.

122 - The stone-fitting work in Ollantaytambo's Temple of the Sun shows great skill. It is thought that the Incas employed the renowned masons of the Lake Titicaca region for its building.

123 top left - In Ollantaytambo, like in many of royal possessions in the Urubamba Valley, terracing was used for agricultural purposes.

123 top right - The Incas managed to survive during the Spaniards' siege of Ollantaytambo by flooding the plateau beneath the fortress and fortifying themselves upon the summit of the city, protected by the sheer mountain flanks.

123 bottom - This building in Ollantaytambo's lower section demonstrates another Inca building technique: the lower part of the wall is built in stone and the upper part in sun-dried brick or adobe.

HIRAM BINGHAM AND THE MYTH OF MACHU PICCHU

"Suddenly, we found ourselves in the midst of a series of buildings covered by jungle growth. Their walls were made of a beautiful white granite, splendidly cut and worked so as to join together perfectly without the need of cement. This site reserved us one surprise after another! We soon realized that we were in the midst of the most beautiful ruins to have ever been found in Peru." In this way, the North American explorer, Hiram Bingham, the leader of a Yale University expedition, described the initial impact of the ruins of Machu Picchu, which were destined to become one of the world's most famous archaeological sites. Bingham's discovery occurred on July 24th, 1911, after he had received some indications from some local farmers.

The next year, after receiving substantial financing from Yale University and from the National Geographic Society, Bingham returned to Machu Picchu and initiated what is often remembered as one of the first interdisciplinary scientific expeditions in Peru. Its enormous success indirectly fueled the fame of other Inca ruins and, at that time, photographs of them taken by celebrated Peruvian photographer, Martín Chambi, were published throughout the world.

Located northwest of the city of Cuzco, Machu Picchu stands at an altitude of 9270 ft (2850 m) above the Vilcanota River valley, on two mountain peaks called respectively Huayna Picchu (the young peak) and Machu Picchu (the old peak). This citadel was the property of the sovereign, Pachacutec and at the same time the main site of a network of royal properties built along the Capac Ñan – the Royal Trail – to exploit the riches of the Vilcanota River valley (Vilcanota was the name given to the upper part of the Urubamba river) and to get prestigious goods for the royal Inca and his *panaca*.

Archaeologists believe that Machu Picchu was built between 1450 and 1470 AD and abandoned after the fall of Tupac Amaru, the last Inca rebel, in 1572.

The city is divided into two large sectors: the urban sector to the north and the farming sector to the south. The area to the north is, in turn, divided into two parts: an upper half or *hanan* and a lower half or *hurin*, divided by a central piazza with an elongated shape. Since this was a residential area for the elite, a good number of the Picchu structures are comprised of buildings which reflect Andean architectural traditions. These include the *cancha*, which is a sort of small piazza with only one access surrounded by three or four one- or two-story buildings, with a double-slanted roof made of perishable materials. These, the most refined of the Inca structures, were accompanied by other less finished structures, without patios and probably built to house servants or *yanaconas*.

The probable residence of the royal Inca himself has also been identified. It is located in the Temple of the Sun area (the Torreón) and its entrance is controlled by a series of barriers. Its walls and the stone used for their building are of a much higher quality than those of the other elite residences.

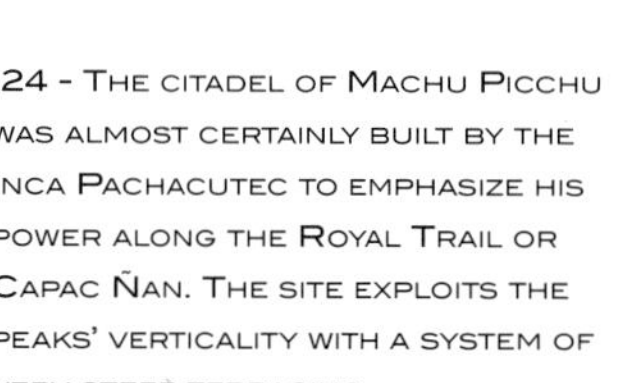

124 - The citadel of Machu Picchu was almost certainly built by the Inca Pachacutec to emphasize his power along the Royal Trail or Capac Ñan. The site exploits the peaks' verticality with a system of very steep terracing.

125 - Machu Picchu, in the lush Urubamba Valley, is located northwest of Cuzco at 9359 ft (2850 m) is built upon two rocky peaks called Huayna Picchu (the young peak) and Machu Picchu (the old peak) respectively.

A series of canals brought spring water to it directly so that those residing there were provided with water in its purest form. From there, the water flowed on to serve the rest of the citadel through a series of complex canals and fountains; the system forms is one of the most interesting features of Machu Picchu.

In addition to its residential buildings, the Picchu ensemble included an enormous concentration of temples. These include: the Temple of the Sun (with a perfectly curved wall resembling the one in the Coricancha), the Intihuatana Temple,

the Temple of the Three Windows and, in the eastern sub-sector, the Condor Temple. The Intihuatana Temple was probably a solar clock used for a complex system of astronomical measurements that determined the start and end of farming periods. In Bingham's view, however, the Temple of Three Windows served for the celebration of the *Tambotoco*, the three windows through which Manco Capac and his brothers came, near Pacaritambo after the god Viracocha had completed the creation.

The extreme refinement of the Picchu structures and their excellent state of preservation (even though, it should be noted, many buildings were reconstructed with a heavy hand soon after their discovery) make Picchu the icon of the "lost city" concept. Its extraordinary features include its perfect construction at a site where nature and the man-made splendidly merge together. The city's architecture is magnificently adapted to the astonishing differences in the levels of terrain through the use of a terrace-system which includes more than one hundred terraces with ramps connecting the citadel's various sectors. This site, beautifully set in luxuriant mountain greenery, must have been seen as a sacred and special place and specifically selected. Its two peaks were objects of veneration and pilgrimages, and the Incas built ceremonial structures on them. Even the rock comprising the mountain was a *huaca*; the temple structure was merely a sort of fence built around these natural sacred objects to emphasize their importance. Here, the Inca Pachacutec found the perfect place to celebrate his divine origin and powers.

126 top - In Machu Picchu one can see the *cancha* structure, the stone enclosure surrounding Inca houses. The tops of the walls in the shape of truncated triangles were used to hold the wooden-frame, straw-thatched roofs.

126 bottom - Ramps, stairs and doors allow for movement between terraces.

127 - Numerous ceremonial structures exist in the city, as well as an area where the Inca and his *panaqa* resided. Houses and warehouses are also present.

128-129 - The city's principal square is the largest flat open space. The prevalently agricultural sector extends to south; the urban one to north.

PACHACUTEC'S EXPANSIONIST POLICY

Once he had consolidated his rule over the Cuzco region, Pachacutec embarked on an aggressive expansionist policy that included lengthy military campaigns. The result was that during his reign the Incas achieved domination over a great part of what is present-day Peru. The young Topa Inca Yupanqui accompanied his father Pachacutec on these campaigns, and many of the military successes of the period are attributed to him.

We have already seen how under the reign of Viracocha, the eighth Inca, many alliances were made with the chiefs around Lake Titicaca. This area held great interest for the Incas because, besides being rich in natural resources, it was a gateway to the southern Andean area and to its mines (the region of Potosí in Bolivia, northern Chile and Argentina) and to the lowlands of Bolivia, with its vast *cocales* (coca plantations; this herb was used to alleviate exhaustion, hunger and for ceremonial purposes). It was, in fact, specifically the Titicaca area which most interested Pachacutec but its conquest came only after he managed to defeat the powerful kingdom of Qolla and its leader, Ciuchi Capac. Historical sources, however, are not clear about the chronology of this conquest and whether it took place before or after the other two important military campaigns led by Pachacutec and his son toward the north and the western coast and toward the eastern Amazon area.

For their conquest of the northwestern area, the Incas used troops recruited from the newly subjugated Chanca. The Incas soon managed to overcome the resistance shown by the various ethnic groups which barred rapid advancement to the north. Pachacutec and his son halted their campaign only after having occupied the fertile kingdom of Cajamarca, governed by Cuismancu Capac. This kingdom was located more than 620 miles (1000 km) from Cuzco, in the northern Peruvian sierra. From here, the Incas took advantage of their position to rid themselves of Cajamarca's most powerful ally, the Chimú kingdom; this extended over hundreds of square miles on the northern coast around present-day Lima. According to some chroniclers, a Pachacutec's general used a stratagem to take the two allies, Cuismancu Capac and Minchaçaman, the king of the Chimú, prisoner.

130 - Pachacutec extended his lands north to the realm of Cajamarca, which had a pre-Inca tradition of manufacturing kaolin pottery (Museum für Völkerkunde, Vienna).

131 - In his march south Pachacutec ran into the powerful groups in the Lake Titicaca zone, including the Qolla, who built funerary towers in the city of Sillustani.

132 left - From Paramonga it was possible to dominate the Pativilca river valley.

132-133 - The fortress of Paramonga was perhaps a Chimú outpost in the Pativilca region.

133 - Built on overlapping four terraces with adobe walls reinforced with stones, Paramonga was probably a defensive building but perhaps also had a public/ceremonial function.

THE CHIMÚ KINGDOM

According to myth, the Chimú kingdom and its splendid capital built of adobe was founded by the semi-divine hero, Taycanamo, who came from the sea. A dynasty of nine governors, who ruled the northern coast of Peru and almost the entire Piura area valley on the Ecuador border, is said to have descended from this mythological hero. This desert kingdom soon became a significant obstacle to Inca ambitions and we know that, at the height of its splendor, the kingdom of Chimú was equal in extent to the Inca kingdom and occupied about 620 miles (1000 km) of coastline. Between 1460 and 1480, the ninth sovereign, Minchaçaman, was defeated by the Children of the Sun. They had a powerful desire for control over this area which, even though

134-135 AND 135 - IN ADDITION TO THE HOMES OF THE ELITE, CHAN CHAN ALSO HAD VARIOUS CEREMONIAL COMPLEXES, AMONG WHICH WAS THE IMPOSING HUACA DEL DRAGON, ORNAMENTED WITH FRIEZES WHICH DEPICT A CAT-SHAPED BEING. THIS DESERT CAPITAL IS COMPLETELY BUILT WITH SUN DRIED-MUD BRICKS OR *ADOBE*.

134 BOTTOM - IN THIS MODEL OF ONE OF THE PALACES IN CHAN CHAN, MADE IN WOOD AND SHELL INLAYS, A HIGH-RANKING FIGURE SITS ON A THRONE UNDER A CANOPY. THE BUILDING IS DECORATED WITH A FRIEZE OF FISH. THE ARTIFACT BELONGS TO THE CHIMÚ CULTURE, WHICH FLOURISHED BETWEEN THE 11TH AND 14TH CENTURIES (MAAHUN, TRUJILLO).

desert, had been radically transformed by the immense hydraulic operations carried out by the Chimú. In fact, it is estimated that thanks to the construction of aqueducts and embankments for the channeling of water, the Chimú were able to gain agricultural land that covered double the surface area available today – even with the advantage of modern farming technologies. In this regard, it should be noted that the Chimú governors, just like the Inca, managed to organize a collective work force to maintain this imposing hydraulic system without which a large part of the population would not have had enough food and resources for survival.

Chimú's capital city, Chan Chan, along with the majestic pyramids in the northern part of the kingdom, which include Sipán and Tucume, today provide us with the most evident testimonial of the splendor of the past. The city is built of adobe, reeds and mud (*quincha*) and of large blocks of dried mud (*adobones*). These are in an optimal state of conservation because of the dry coastal climate. In addition, this ancient kingdom is famous for its splendid reliefs portraying gods and the Chimú animal reign.

The heirs of a very refined and millenary artistic tradition, the Chimú were also exceptional weavers and particularly skillful in creating feather inserts and gold work. After their conquest, the Incas deported many of the local master craftsmen to Cuzco to serve the imperial court there.

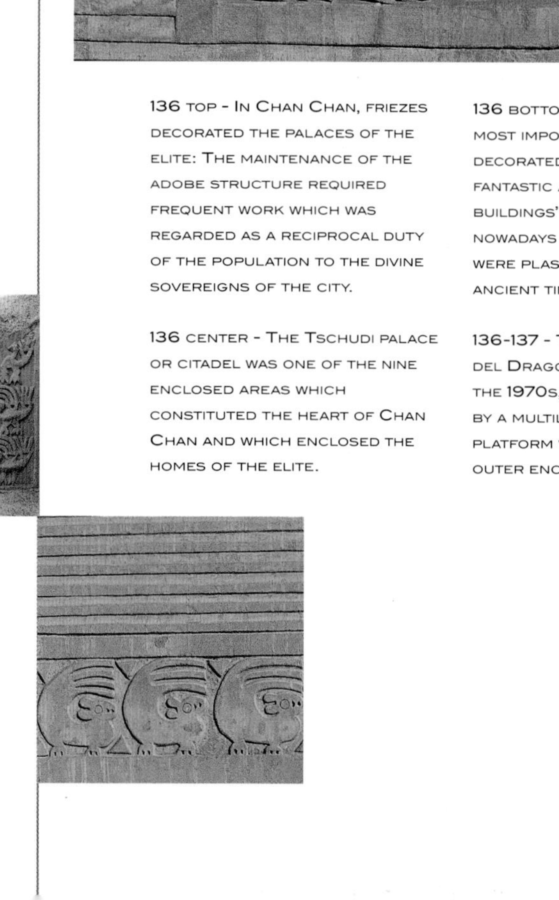

136 top - In Chan Chan, friezes decorated the palaces of the elite: The maintenance of the adobe structure required frequent work which was regarded as a reciprocal duty of the population to the divine sovereigns of the city.

136 center - The Tschudi palace or citadel was one of the nine enclosed areas which constituted the heart of Chan Chan and which enclosed the homes of the elite.

136 bottom - The walls of the most important buildings were decorated with friezes of both fantastic and real animals. The buildings' decorations, nowadays of a sandy color, were plastered and colored in ancient times.

136-137 - The Huaca del Dragon, restored during the 1970s, is a complex formed by a multilevel central platform within an outer enclosure.

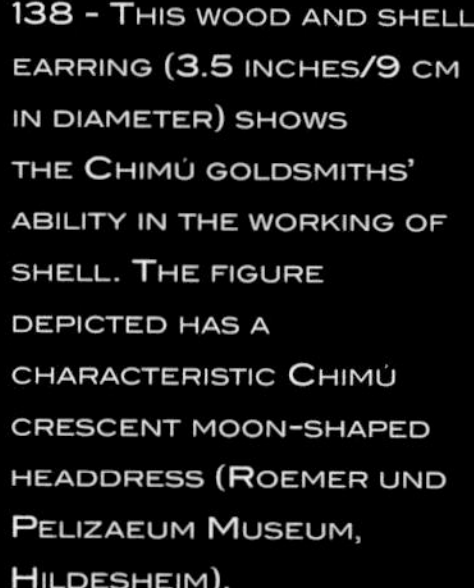

138 - This wood and shell earring (3.5 inches/9 cm in diameter) shows the Chimú goldsmiths' ability in the working of shell. The figure depicted has a characteristic Chimú crescent moon-shaped headdress (Roemer und Pelizaeum Museum, Hildesheim).

139 left - The Chimú produced a large quantity of painted wood ceremonial statues, like this one in Carrubo (Maahun, Trujillo)

139 right - This vase's wooden base depicts a figure on a throne (Roemer und Pelizaeum Museum, Hildesheim).

140 - This tapestry depicts a Chimú figure with the characteristic crescent-shaped headdress. He is holding two staffs (Museo Nacional de Arqueología, Antropología e Historia

141 - The Chimú often depicted cats which, in this fabric, alternate with figures wearing crescent-shaped headdresses (Museo Nacional de Arqueología, Antropología e Historia

142 - This ornament depicts a figure wearing a crescent-shaped headdress; the robe was probably enriched with decorations made of precious metals. The man is holding a ceremonial cup (North Coast of Peru, Sicán-Lambayeque culture, 11th -13th centuries) (Gold Museum, Lima).

143 - Gold masks are a characteristic feature of the luxury gods produced on Peru's north coast. They were used as grave goods. This specimen, covered with cinnabar, belongs to the Sicán-Lambayeque culture of the 11th-13th centuries (Gold Museum, Lima).

144 - Sicán-lambayeque iceremonial cups (11th-13th centuries) made with precious metals and offered as grave goods are similar to those used during the ceremonies (Gold Museum, Lima).

145 - Cups of the Sicán-Lambayeque culture had various decorations depending on their use. This vase's anthropomorphic being with feline features perhaps alludes to a deity (Gold Museum, Lima).

TOPA INCA YUPANQUI'S REIGN

After the conquest of Chimú, Pachacutec relinquished his position as commander of the army and conferred the greater part of his power on his son, Topa Yupanqui, beginning the custom of a ruler appointing the successor to the throne of the *sapay* Inca (the sole Inca), during his lifetime.

After the fall of Cajamarca and of Chan Chan, hotspots of rebellion began to be seen in various areas of the conquered lands. A number of accounts record uprisings among ethnic groups living in the Lake Titicaca region, and it seems certain that the Incas had to spend much energy in keeping these areas under control.

The Inca conquest of the southern coast of Peru came about in various stages both through military campaigns and through trade with the local rulers. According to the chronicler Bernabé de Cobo (1653), the army was already exhausted as a result of many years of battles and also was also not very capable of fighting in the coastal region because of its different environmental conditions and very hot climate.

It is probable that at least the conquest of the lords of Chincha (on the southern coast of Lima) was achieved in a relatively peaceful way. A valuable report from the colonial period – valuable because it is living testimony of the techniques used to peacefully subjugate peoples – tells us how events unfolded. Though it is possible that much earlier events are being described, the report recounts that one of Pachacutec's generals, on reaching the Chincha Valley, declared that he had come to bring gifts and fabrics to the local lords and that he had no intention of ravaging the area becasue the Inca kingdom was already very powerful.

In accepting these gifts, the local lords decided to recognize the magnificence of the Children of the Sun and soon afterwards the Incas, if not gaining lands, gained a skillful work force. It was made up mainly of women, the so-called *mamaconas*, who were skilled in preparing the fabrics which served as widely sought after trade goods during the period of the Inca conquests and which satisfied the needs of the Inca court. Pachacutec gradually gained additional privileges including farmlands and the right to build administrative settlements to control the flow of tribute coming from this area.

It is more probable, however, that this "peaceful penetration" strategy pertained to the conquest of the Cañete area, where the lord of the Huarco opposed the invaders with fierce resistance. To provide a logistical base for his army, Topa Yupanqui was obliged to found a military settlement. This later became an actual city: Incahuasi (In the Quechua language this means "house of the Inca," a generic name for many Inca settlements probably founded in the area after its conquest). This city was the largest Inca settlement on the southern coast but it was evidently built with great urgency, as the rough architecture seems to suggest. This can be seen in most of the low walls visible in the site, but not in the most refined *canchas*, probably destined to house officers.

At the end of Pachacutec's reign and during that of Topa Yupanqui expeditions were launched toward the Amazon. The bellicose tribes of the forest were a real nightmare for the Inca who never ventured to conquer their lands, which were harsh and unfit for their troops. We do not know exactly how far armies from Cuzco penetrated into the Amazon region: several sources report the conquest of immense territories east of Lake Titicaca, and some chroniclers suggest that in navigating the Madre de Dios river, the Incas went as far as the border between Bolivia and Brazil. The expeditions toward the Amazon were unsuccessful; however, despite the fact that the Incas described the Amazonian peoples as wild and untamable (a recurring *topos* with which the Inca described the populations they were not able to control), they continued interacting with them to trade luxury goods such as bird feathers, exotic animals and skins.

During the reign of Pachacutec it seems that the Inca managed to reach Ecuador, even though the story of the conquest of that region is still very controversial; in fact, it is traditionally attributed to Huayna Capac, the son of Topa Yupanqui.

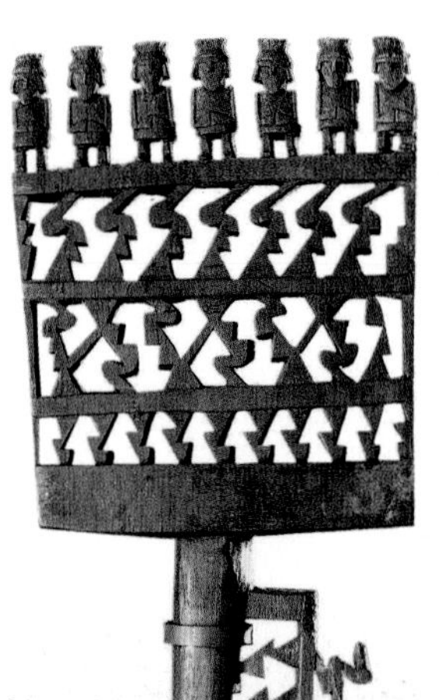

146 - THIS ICA-CHINCA CEREMONIAL OAR (715 FT/218 M) IN HEIGHT IS DECORATED WITH A FRIEZE OF BIRD-LIKE BEINGS. DURING THE CONQUEST OF THE CENTRAL SOUTHERN COAST OF PERU, THE INCAS CAME UP AGAINST EFFECTIVE REGIMES (MUSÉE QUAI BRANLY, PARIS).

147 - THIS INCA GOLD FEMALE STATUETTE WEARS A TYPICAL CLOAK HELD BY A BROOCH. SIMILAR STATUETTES HAVE BEEN FOUND IN THE SETTINGS OF CEREMONIAL BURIALS OF GIRLS SACRIFICED TO THE MOUNTAINS (ETHNOLOGISCHES MUSEUM, BERLIN).

INCA SITES ON THE COAST: PURUCHUCO AND TAMBO COLORADO

The Inca build several settlements on the Peruvian coast: some were administrative centers, others military, and still others were others yet *tambos*, or postal stations along the Royal Trail. Puruchuco and Tambo Colorado, two of the most interesting among them, are the subject of recent studies.

Puruchuco, situated within the urban perimeter of the city of Lima, is a good example of provincial Inca architecture, in this case a true and proper fusion between typical structures for the local elite (the so-called *audiencias*, or courts and terraces) and the *canchas*, the basic units which make up the Inca settlements. Puruchuco was the residence of the *curacas* (the ethnic heads) of the area who, after the Inca conquest of the coast, adopted some traditions from the sierra. In the site, build with adobe, one can appreciate elements of imperial architecture such as the triangular niches and portals with double jambs. Coeval with the palatial complex is an enormous cemetery, one of the most important archaeological discoveries of the recent years (2002) in the whole Andean area. Here, a few inches below the sand of the coastal desert, more than 2000 individuals have been found, buried in funerary wrappings (*fardos*), in different layers of fabric arranged to reproduce the human aspect. The archaeologist Guillermo Cock, who is researching on the site, has distinguished the burials of people belonging to the local elite such as the so-called "Cotton King," a person wrapped in more than 295 lbs (135 kg) of rough cotton and with an enormous quantity of accessories, agricultural products (corn, potatoes, beans, pumpkin and lime for chewing coca leaves – which last he was still holding in his hands), shells and clothes. Through this exceptional discovery and through the study of the bodies of many individuals archaeologists hope to efficiently map the Inca presence in the area through the study of their funerary garments. But the cemetery yields much more. The bodies deposited in Puruchuco cover a span of a hundred years, partly contemporary with the Spanish conquest. Many bear the traces of the epidemics that the Europeans brought and their study will help us to understand the impact of the conquest on the Andean territory.

Tambo Colorado is situated south of Lima, in the Pisco Valley. It is believed that the site was built along the Royal Trail, on its coastal branch, which joined Cuzco with Pachacamac (the site of an important oracle), 16.5 miles (30 km) south of Lima, going via the military settlement of Incahuasi.

148 - THE SITE OF TAMBO COLORADO PRESENTS THE FUSION OF STYLIZED INCA ARCHITECTONIC STANDARDS, IN THIS CASE THE TRAPEZOIDAL DOORS AND THE NICHES, WITH THE USE OF ADOBE, THE TRADITIONAL BUILDING MATERIAL OF THE COAST.

148-149 AND 149 TOP - THE ADMINISTRATIVE PALACE AND THE LARGE IRREGULARLY SHAPED PLAZA ARE AMONG THE PRINCIPAL BUILDINGS OF TAMBO COLORADO, A CITY IN THE PISCO VALLEY. THE CITY OWES ITS NAME TO THE LIVELY PAINTINGS WHICH ONCE COVERED ITS WALLS.

This very large settlement is one of the most important Inca administrative centers on the southern coast. It was built, as is often the case for provincial Inca sites, on pre-existing structures built by local groups. Researchers have always been attracted by both the chromatic richness of the paintings which adorn the adobe walls of the site (hence the name Tambo Colorado), and by the fact that the structures, though mainly Inca in form and function, were built using the coastal techniques of adobe and *tapia*.

Though the site was built to control the new lands annexed to the empire during the conquest of the coast, numerous ceremonial structures stand out for their importance, among which the *ushnu*, or ceremonial platform, and the great square of a warped trapezoidal shape, which, according to Anthony F. Aveni and Gary Urton, experts in Andean astronomical matters, was to align its axis to the movement of the stars during particular moments of the calendar.

149 center - Puruchuco was the residence of the *Curacas* (ethnic leaders) of the region who, after the Inca conquest of the coast, adopted some of the *Sierra's* traditions in the building of this important complex.

149 bottom - Puruchuco is a provincial Inca site, where the typical structures of the local elite's architecture (the so-called *Audiencias*, i.e., courts and terraces) fuse with the *canchas*, the basic structures which make up the Inca settlements.

THE CONSOLIDATION OF THE EMPIRE: HUAYNA CAPAC

Topa Yupanqui died in 1493 as a result of a conspiracy. He was succeeded by his young son, Huayna Capac. The new ruler focused on consolidating the conquests of the past and on reaffirming his own dominion – both physical and symbolic – over the territories conquered by his predecessors. Among his most important campaigns was that against the Chachapoyas, an ethnic group organized in lordships which occupied the northeast of the country in the Marañon area, an endeavor that required two year-long campaigns. Among Huayna Capac's achievements, according to the Spanish chroniclers – particularly Cieza de León – are listed the lengthy and costly campaigns to gain the lands at the extreme northern end of the Inca territory and in Ecuador.

Using Tumipampa (Tomebamba) as a maintenance and supply base, the Inca army tried more than once to penetrate the area. They were not very successful in doing so. As at other times, when the campaign became basically a series of guerilla skirmishes rather than battles and the population took shelter in the dense forests, the invading Incas could not achieve any realistic victories against them. The battles against the Otavalo and the Caranqui were particularly violent – and the even the capable Huayna Capac risked ending up a prisoner. Only the strong resistance put up by his personal guard of five Cuzco nobles saved him from this fate. However, with the help of fresh troops from Cuzco, the Incas finally managed to conquer the fortress that was the center of resistance for the local populations, who had formed a defensive alliance. This attack was so violent that the lake near the forest (today known as the lagoon of Yahuarcocha) was tinted red from the blood of the fallen.

Huayna Capac established himself in Tumipampa (today, Cuenca), an area that his father had previously conquered and which he considered to be a second mother country because he had been born there. This city was soon to become one of the most important Inca sites in the area north of Tawantinsuyu, together with Ingapirca.

Tumipampa was originally a settlement of the Cañari, the local ethnic group, but later Huayna Capac rebaptized it as Tumipampa, a name derived from that of the *panaca* he belonged to in Cuzco. The city was constructed to reflect Cuzco both in terms of its layout and in the attempt to encircle it with sacred sites, like those that surrounded the capital of the Inca world. The newcomers renamed the local mountains, giving them the same names as the most important sacred peaks in the holy valley of the navel of their world. For this reason, near to today's Cuenca we find a mountain named Huanacauri. This site was immortalized in stone by the mythological Ayar, the brothers of Manco Capac who accompanied him in his conquest of the Cuzco valley. Some chroniclers say that the idol in the local Temple of the Sun was cast in a similar way to the one in Cuzco and that even some of the stones used in the construction of the most important buildings came directly from the Urubamba area.

Notwithstanding the fact that Huayna Capac and his army had established themselves in the area in an almost permanent way, native resistance had not been completely vanquished. The tribal chief of the Cañari, Pinta, managed to escape capture for a very long time and inflicted continuous raids on the Incas in an attempt to wrest his lands from them. However, in 1523 Pinta was finally captured and local resistance suffered a great setback. Punishment for the rebels was designed to set an example: Pinta, a Cañari noble, was skinned alive and his skin used to make a drum to celebrate the Sun God.

Huayna Capac carried out other military events worthy of note; they included expansion of the southern borders of Inca lands in the Chilean area and the pacification of revolts in Bolivia (this was in fact achieved by his generals while the sovereign was occupied with stabilizing his conquests in Ecuador).

Huayna Capac died in 1528, possibly in Quito or in Tumipamba, and his son Ninan Cuyuchi also died at the same time. This beset the Inca Empire with the chaos and turmoil that resulted from a war of succession. The sovereign had been stricken with a hemorrhagic fever, though some scholars claim he died a violent death caused by poisoning. In any case, hemorrhagic fever was causing numerous deaths among the local populations. It seems that smallpox and German measles had reached the Andean peoples for the first time and they had no immunity or defense against them. These diseases were brought into the New World by the Spanish who were exploring the South American coast with a view to making additional landings so that after their successes in Mexico they could add other territories to the list of conquests made for the Spanish crown.

151 LEFT - THE INCAS' CONQUEST OF ECUADOR INVOLVED ENCOUNTERS WITH THE POWERFUL LORDSHIPS OF THE NORTH, WHICH INCLUDED THE OTAVALO AND THE CARANQUI (PRIVATE COLLECTION).

151 RIGHT - A POTTERY TRADITION DEVELOPED AMONG THE CARANQUI THAT WAS CHARACTERIZED BY PORTRAITS OF MEN HOLDING COMMANDING POSITIONS (BANCO CENTRAL MUSEUM, QUITO).

INGAPIRCA: AN INCA SETTLEMENT AT THE EXTREME NORTHERN END OF THE EMPIRE

At Ingapirca, little farther north of Tumibamba, the Incas remodeled another local settlement to be used as an outpost of their presence in the turbulent province of the Cañars. Because of the Tumipampa settlement's closeness to the northern capital, Ingapirca was probably not an important administrative center; however, it was strongly imbued with symbolism for the local peoples and the Incas wanted to occupy it to reaffirm their presence in key places in the Cañari area.

The Incas built their new structures to include many from the prior settlement, and the result was an interesting and typical combination which marked Inca architecture in the provinces. The extreme flexibility of their architecture can be particularly appreciated here because of the skillful arrangement of the site. It unites structures that had a typically local layout (including the so-called Castillo) with structures typical of Inca administrative

cities (including the *colcas* or warehouses, the *canchas* and the farming terraces). The Castillo is an oval-shaped structure which is representative of traditional Cañari architecture. It stands on an outcrop of steep natural rock, painted red on one side; it is considered sacred by the local peoples who "offer" the rock numerous sacrifices. Although today only traces of the Inca structures and their underlying predecessors remain, archaeologists have brought to light the tomb of an important woman; she was accompanied by many servants and by a rich array of funerary artifacts which date back to the era of Cañari independence.

152 - Inca structures in Ingapirca encompass an earlier settlement: the result is an interesting fusion typical of Inca building techniques in the provinces.

152-153 - Ingapirca is an Inca outpost in the turbulent province of the Cañars, symbol of the conquest of Ecuador which occurred in the Huayna Capac era.

153 bottom - The Castillo is an egg-shaped building typical of Cañari architecture. It was encompassed by the architecture of the Inca conquerors.

THE CIVIL WAR AND THE SPANISH CONQUEST

155 - The complex ornament of the Chimú era is a *naringuera* (6.4 inches/16.5 cm high) which was attached to the nose and hung down in front of the wearer's mouth. (Rautenstrauch-Joest Museum, Cologne).

156 - This Inca era male stone head (15.3 inches/39 cm) was found in Cuzco's Amarucancha enclosure, where the palace of the Inca ruler Huayna Capac had once stood. It perhaps depicted the sovereign's portrait or that of an idealized Inca ruler (Museo de América, Madrid).

THE STRUGGLE FOR THE THRONE: ATAHUALLPA AND HUASCAR

Upon the death of Huayna Capac and of his son Ninan Cuyuchi, a conflict broke out – the worst in Inca history – over the succession to the throne. Though the nobles closest to Huayna Capac had attempted to conceal his death to avoid setting off feuds and the resulting vendettas among the various *panacas* in support of their candidates, his death was secret for only a short time. The Spanish, however, were able to profit from the civil war – which divided the Andean peoples and brought chaos to the area. Thus, the Spanish made an astonishingly quick conquest of Tawantinsuyu with only a handful of men.

Atahuallpa and Huascar, the two rivals for the throne, were both sons of Huayna Capac, but had different mothers. Huayna Capac had appointed first Ninan Cuyuchi and then Atahuallpa (the two sons who had accompanied him on his campaign in Ecuador) to succeed him to the throne. But, later on, he appointed Huascar. Another source, however, says that Huayna Capac had selected Huascar as his second choice to even though the priests' forecasts about him were so terrible that they had visited Huayna Capac in an attempt to convince him to change his mind. They were not in time; he died immediately after his nomination of Huascar. Whether or not Atahuallpa was the "chosen one," he nonetheless probably at first renounced the throne. In fact, Huascar had himself crowned very quickly, thanks to intercession by his mother, Raura Ocllo, who – as soon as she learned of the death of her husband, Huayna Capac in Ecuador – immediately traveled to Cuzco, where Huascar was governor, to convince him to take advantage of this favorable moment to wear the coveted *mazcaypaycha* (royal crown). In any case, Atahuallpa, even though he had recognized his half-brother as the sole Inca, had remained at the head of the powerful northern army stationed in Ecuador. Huascar, feeling unsure of himself because of the survival of another potential and legitimate rival to the throne, decided to rid himself of Atahuallpa. Up to this point, the story of this contest for the throne, as narrated by chronicler Betanzos, presents Huascar as an ambitious and unscrupulous man. But, as we have seen, Betanzos was a faithful supporter of Pachacutec and of the *panacas* of *hanan* Cuzco, which also included both Atahuallpa and Huascar. In any case, immediately after his election, Huascar took the dangerous decision of distancing himself from the *panacas* of *hanan* Cuzco because these nobles, in his opinion, were too powerful and too intent on influencing his government. As a result, he openly favored the families of the *hurin* half of Cuzco. Other chroniclers, however, imply that Atahuallpa's intentions were not very clear during this period and that his decision to station himself in the north with his powerful army could be the prelude to the founding of a sort of "new" kingdom in this region. For this reason, Huascar was very justified in feeling insecure. Perhaps in the beginning Atahuallpa had been willing to recognize the authority of his half-brother but his behavior was ambiguous: Cabello de Balboa tells us how the governor of the province of the Cañars had sent word to Huascar stating that Atahuallpa was accustomed to playing the role of Huayna Capac and that he behaved just like an Inca – possibly encouraged by the generals of Huayna Capac who considered him to be the most skillful of sovereigns. This situation fueled the conflict to an even greater extent, and Huascar soon sought open warfare against his rival. In fact, he ordered the torture and execution of all the many messengers that Atahuallpa sent him in homage following his election. Huascar invited General Atoq (meaning "fox") to oppose the troops of Atahuallpa in the north but Atahuallpa, in turn, attempted to defend his position by sending out an army under the leadership of General Quizquiz. These armies confronted each other near Chillopampa and Atoq won, but only momentarily. Some sources say that Atoq, thanks to the help of the Cañars, who were full of resentment over the invasion of Atahuallpa's armies, managed to capture Atahuallpa. They held him prisoner in Tumipampa, from where he managed to escape by changing into a snake. This miraculous episode, which presents Atahuallpa as a protégé of the gods, was obviously passed on to the Spanish by indigenous informers favorable to this sovereign to celebrate his deeds. We do not know whether Atahuallpa was really caught and, in case, in what manner he managed to escape. In any case, Atahuallpa reordered his troops: being able to count on fresh strengths from Quito, he won this second round. Atoq was caught and his body torn to pieces as a sign of the anger of the generals of the northern army. Without losing any more time and leveraging the success he just gained, Atahuallpa had himself crowned *sapay* Inca in Tumipampa. At this point he began marching south with his army, probably intent on a conclusive challenge with his half-brother. As custom dictated in the Andean world, Atahuallpa could not face such a crucial phase of his life without consulting a powerful oracle to predict his future. Being near Huamachuco, he consulted Catequil, one of the most powerful *huacas* at the time, who resided in that area. Catequil correctly predicted the destruction of the Inca people within a few years. This unleashed Atahuallpa's fury and he devastated Catequil's sanctuary, thereby in the eyes if the local population committing a greast sacrilege. In the meantime, Huascar was reorganizing his army to respond to the then imminent arrival of the northern armies.

ATAHUALLPA, INCA XIIII.

158 - This anonymous painting of the early colonial era portrays the Inca Atahuallpa (Ethnologisches Museum, Berlin).

159 - Huascar, here depicted as the Inca, was killed on his brother's orders at the end of a long civil war (Ethnologisches Museum, Berlin).

SOCIAL AND TAX ORGANIZATION IN THE PROVINCES

At the top of the Inca social pyramid was the sovereign, and immediately below the priests (often his relatives) and the noble families (the *panacas*). Non-Inca nobility also enjoyed great prestige, like the "Incas de privilegio" who represented the elite of the non-Inca populations of the Cuzco area, and the provincial elite (the so-called *curacas*). But most of the people population was made up of farmers and shepherds residing in the provinces. Inca society was based on a strict control of this populace, which was organized on a decimal system, on which the calculation of taxes was also based.

The smallest group of ruled populations or tributaries was called a *chunca* (10 family groups) and the biggest unit was called a *huno* (10,000 family groups). The organization of the population provided, therefore, the basis for the exaction of the taxes which were due to the Inca. It also allowed for the organization of the work shifts (*mita*) and of the time every adult male had to spend in the army. All the provinces paid tributes: when the Inca conquered a new land, the first thing was a census of the population so as to calculate what the province would have had to "pay." Whatever the population's pre-existing local organization system, the decimal system was imposed upon them, and a tribute of periods of work was demanded. This naturally translated as agricultural goods or products of various kinds. Land itself was only rarely expropriated, but families had to allocate part of its products to the Inca, and could keep only part of the fruit of their toil for themselves. The products allocated to the Inca were generally stored in state depositories, present in the provinces and cities of Inca foundation (the *llacta*). At the beginning of the conquest, the Spanish came across numerous *llactas* with deposits (*colcas*) full of all kinds of produce from the provinces.

Each local *curaca* was responsible for managing the system, even though there was an Inca governor for each province. Helped by his lieutenants and the *quipucamayoc* (accountants who recorded the tributes on *quipu* or knotted strings), he controlled the flow of goods from the province.

It would be too discursive to go into the details of the social organization of the provinces, in part because the situation differed according to the territory, and we do not know how successfully the Inca were able to implement their intent to move all the people into a single system.

There was at least one important division in the mass of the population: between those who offered a specialized

160 LEFT - THE FELINE-FEATURED PESTLE (3.4 INCHES/8.8 CM IN HEIGHT) ILLUSTRATES INCA ART'S TASTE FOR LINEARITY (MUSEO DE AMÉRICA, MADRID).

160 RIGHT - THE PESTLE WITH TWO CATS ON THE HANDLES WAS USED FOR RITUAL PURPOSES (MUSEO DE AMÉRICA, MADRID).

service (the *camayoc*), and those who went on work shifts (*mitayoc*) and from whom a low level of specialization was demanded. Some accounts of the period which immediately followed the conquest tell us about how life worked in some of the administrative units and their tasks. In some cases, if one administrative unit was made up of 100 families (the so-called *pachaca*), 50 families were assigned to permanent service for the Inca, and they could also be relocated to far lands (becoming *mitmae*, the forced emigrants of the empire). The other 50 would have to serve the state on shifts without being relocated, unless they had temporary tasks far from their places of origin (e.g., military service).

The systematic deportation of the population took place for reasons not merely economic: sometimes, following a war, the locals were wiped out and it was therefore necessary to replace them with other people, ideally more obedient and less bellicose. Sometimes, instead, specialized workers were deported. To uproot parts of a population from their homes, from their *huacas* and their ethnic group, was undoubtedly one of the heaviest levies of the Inca dominion, and a reason for resentment which the Spanish were astute in using to their advantage to conquer the territory.

161 left - The silver corncob was used to ensure the fields' fertility. Gardens around the Coricancha in Cuzco had precious-metal replicas of useful plants; they were used in rites performed to promote and ensure fertility (Ethnologisches Museum, Berlin).

161 right - In these illustrations taken from Guaman Poma de Ayala's *Chronicle*, farmers are seen working on potato and maize fields. A large part of the Andean population ate potatoes and maize as their basic food.

TRAVAXA

ZARA PAPA APAICVIAIMO

162 - Agricultural goods were stored in well-designed buildings (from Guaman Poma de Ayala's *Chronicle*).

163 - Llamas were used to carry goods as well as for their meat and their wool. This silver llama carries cloth on its back (American Museum of Natural History, New York).

THE MARCH ON CUZCO AND ATAHUALLPA'S VICTORY

The decisive clashes that brought about Atahuallpa's victory took place on Ecuadorian soil and in the north of Peru. They cost both sides heavy losses. As Atahuallpa gained ground in his southward advance, he also managed to gain more soldiers, including deserters from Huascar's side.

Demoralized by numerous defeats and by the negative responses of the oracles, Huascar decided to lead part of his army in person. A pitched battle took place near Hatun Xauxa (Yanamarca valley) in the central Andes. Atahuallpa's armies prevailed and continued their march toward the capital. In the later episodes of this war, which was by then being conducted on the whole territory north of Cuzco, Huascar, in leading his army, revealed all his inexperience as a warrior. He soon fell into the hands of Atahuallpa's generals, Quizquiz and Challcochima. These two, having captured Huascar, had some of their troops dress up as Cuzco soldiers and march toward an area where many of Huascar's men were stationed. At that point, Challcochima ordered his men to reveal their true identity. Then, seeing their captive king and realizing that part of the army was wiped out, the rest of Huascar's troops panicked, broke ranks and ran away.

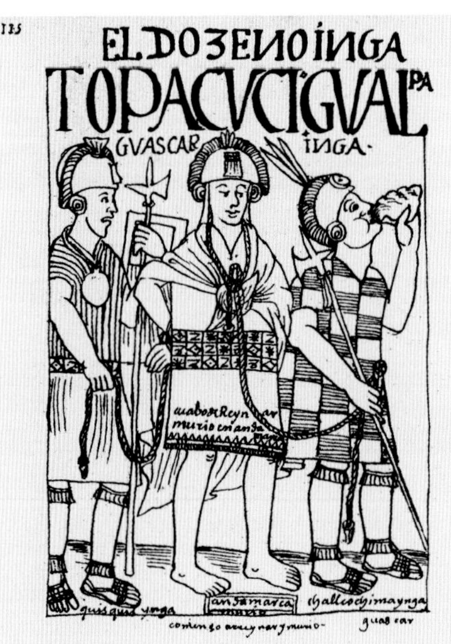

With Huascar captured, resistance ended and generals Quizquiz and Challcochima entered Cuzco victoriously, carrying out the revenge that Atahuallpa had ordered, killing all of Huascar's supporters and the members of his *panaca*. Only two of his sons escaped the carnage, Manco Inca and Paullu, who were to play roles in the post-Conquest history. After this, the dignitaries of the *panacas* and their extended family groups (*ayllus*) were forced to pay homage to the double statue of Atahuallpa, a gold idol (*huauque*) on the Yavira mound, near Cuzco.

In the meantime, Atahuallpa was marching toward Cuzco where he would have taken his father's place leading his people. But something interrupted his march: he came to know of a potential new threat to his people. A group of foreigners, whom he had heard about at Huayna Capac's court, after remaining for a while in a village on the extreme north of the Peruvian coast was advancing inland. Atahuallpa did not think of the new arrivals as a true and proper menace, but he thought it important to tackle them and satisfy his curiosity at the same time. He stopped near Cajamarca, where there was a spa now known as the "Inca Baths." His triumph in Cuzco could wait: he ordered his generals to bring his former rival Huascar directly to Cajamarca. The Inca could not imagine that he would never achieve final vengeance, and that he was never to see the center of the Tawantinsuyu again.

164 - In this illustration taken from Guaman Poma de Ayala's *Chronicle*, the Inca Huascar is captured by Atahualpa's soldiers and placed in chains.

165 - Like Huascar, this Moche-era prisoner was of a noble rank, as can be deduced by his enlarged earlobes (Museo de América, Madrid).

TO RECORD WITH KNOTS AND FABRICS: THE QUIPU AND THE TOCAPU

The Andean populations did not have an alphabetic form of writing. In these strongly oral cultures there was, however, a communication system based on three media. The first medium was the *quipu* or knotted strings; the second medium was scroll ornaments (*tocapu*) woven into fabric or painted on vases and on *queros* (wooden cups); the third was painting, which, being the least documented we will skip here.

The first archaeological evidence of these indigenous communication or notation systems has been dated back to the Huari era, but, as usual, most of the information we have regards the Inca period. This is scarce; however, that practically all Inca knowledge was passed on thanks to the reading of the *quipu* and the *tocapu*. Writing with symbols, as in the Andean manner, is called semasiographics, and implies that there is a known reading "code". In the Andean world it was mainly the elite who understood the code and they used the underlying communications for economic and social control to the extent that experts speak of real "political mathematics." Furthermore, there were persons assigned to reading the *quipu*, called *quipucamayoc*. They had the task of interpreting the knots of the *quipu*: the *quipu* was in fact a numerical notation system, but also expressed some concepts. It was based on a series of knots made on woolen or cotton rope (but also, in a few cases, human hair). As the numerical information that one could "write" with knots was very extensive, a knot was not in itself sufficient to fully express a number, so there was another series of details which were expressed within the knot. These were expressed through the direction in which the wool was woven (i.e., twisting to the left or right), its color, the type of knot, and naturally, its position on the rope.

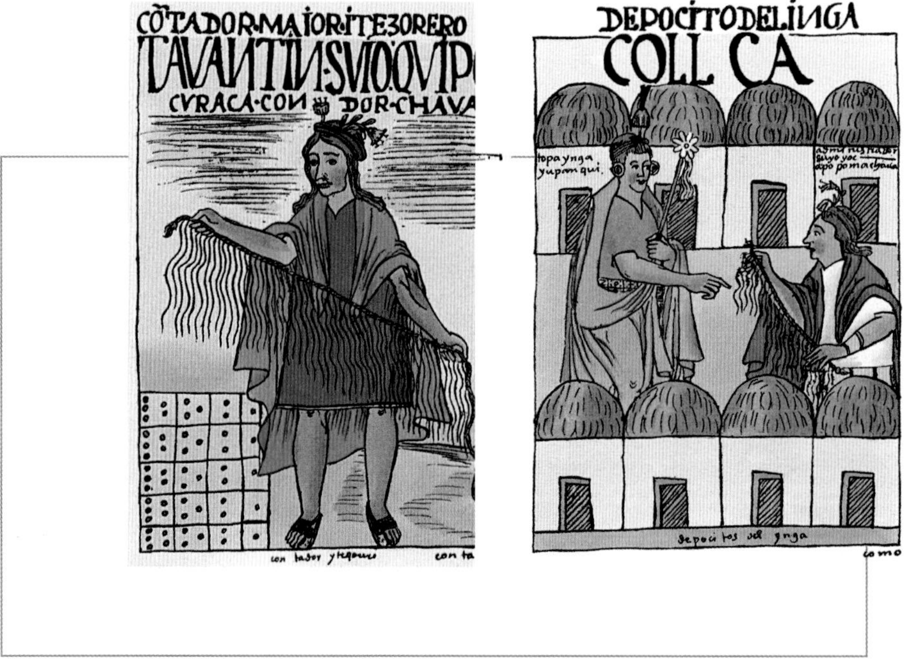

166 LEFT - THIS DRAWING FROM GUAMAN POMA DE AYALA'S *CHRONICLE* DEPICTS A "CONTADOR MAYOR" AND TREASURER OF TAWANTINSUYU WITH A *QUIPU* IN HAND.

166 RIGHT - THE *QUIPUS* WERE A RECORDING DEVICE USED FOR DIFFERENT PURPOSES, AMONG WHICH WAS REGISTRATION OF THE EMPIRE'S RESOURCES, WHICH WERE STORED IN DEPOSITORIES OR *COLCAS*.

Today, most researchers agree that there was a shared system of interpretation for the *quipu* and that they could be interpreted and read by different people, not only by those who had originally made them. In fact, only through accepting this shared interpretation system can we explain how the *quipu* was entrusted with the recording of the complex tributary system of an empire which, at its height encompassed over 770,000 sq. miles (2 million sq. km).

Let us now consider how the basic principle of the numerical reading of the *quipu* worked: the *quipu* is made up of a master rope to which secondary ones are attached. Other auxiliary cords could also be attached to these. On the cords descending from the main one, the knots are distributed at a regular distance in groups. From their position one obtains their numerical value (with a decimal system): the ones closer to the main cord are generally simple knots and indicate thousands and hundreds, those lower down on the strings are generally composed and indicate units.

Only a small number (about 1000) of the *quipus* which must have existed before the conquest have survived. The *quipus* were not destroyed by the Spanish, but during the fighting among the *panacas* in Cuzco, which sought to damage this or that other political faction. The most famous case is that of the destruction of the *quipus* which took place in the war between Atahuallpa and Huascar and the killing of all the *quipucamayoc* in order to perpetrate a definitive *damnatio memoriae* of the losing faction.

During colonial times, when many natives knew how to write in Spanish, they did not give up communicating through images. This is illustrated by the chronicle written by the mixed-race chronicler Guamán Poma de Ayala (*Nueva Córonica y Buen Gobierno*, 1613-15), famous for the richness of the painted tablets accompanying the written narrative.

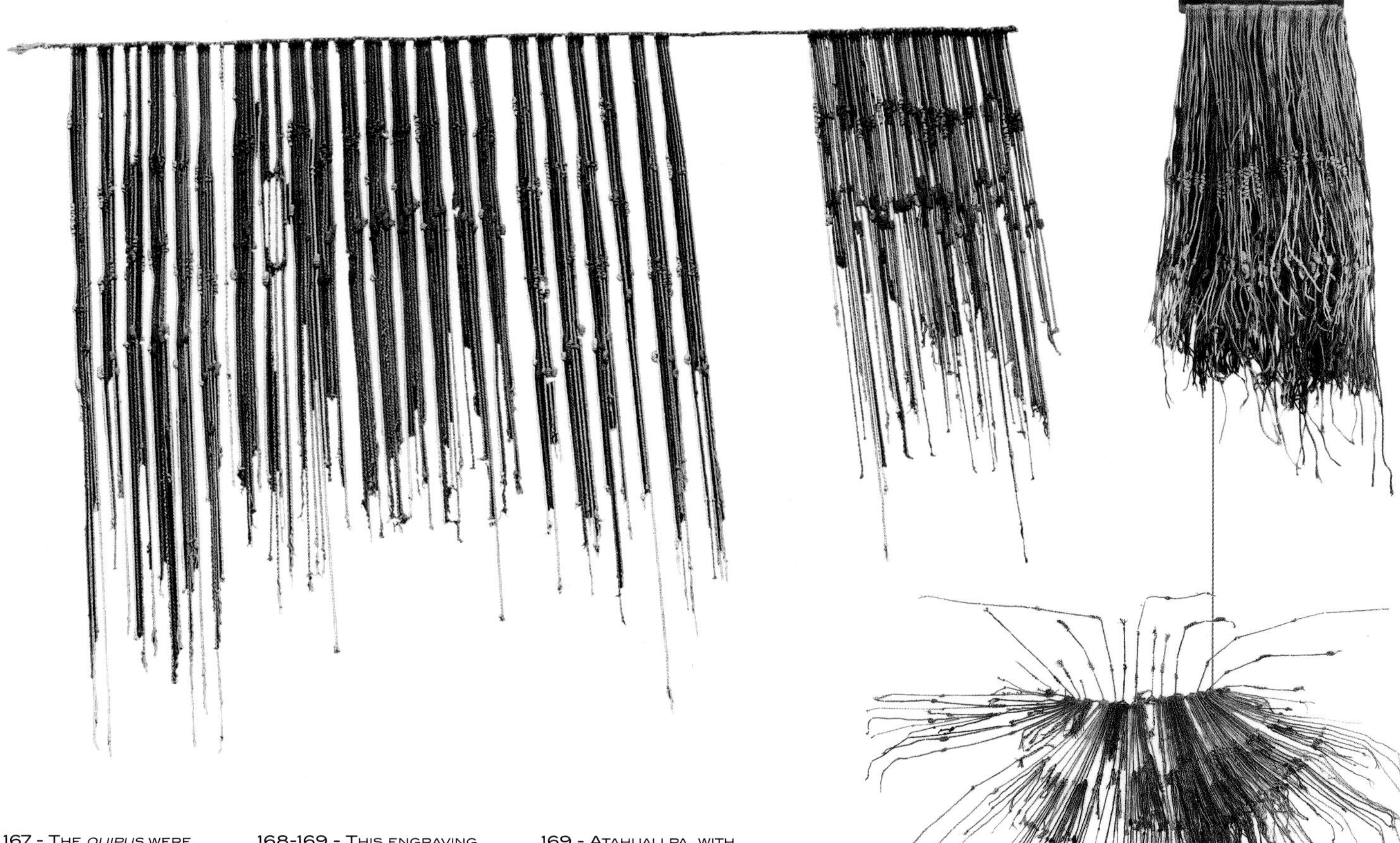

167 - The *quipus* were made of wool, cotton and occasionally of human hair, and could also be used to keep track of the calendar.

168-169 - This engraving from Theodore de Bry's *Americae*, part VI (1596) depicts the encounter between Atahuallpa and Pizarro in Cajamarca.

169 - Atahuallpa, with 25,000 warriors, travels on a litter (sedan-chair) toward Cajamarca to meet Pizarro (Theodore de Bry, *Americae*, part VI, 1596).

THE CAJAMARCA ENCOUNTER

Francisco Pizarro landed on the coast of Peru with a handful of men who were seeking their fortunes. He had made his first surveys when Huayna Capac was still alive, but did not make his first real landing until 1532, when he stationed himself and his men in the city of San Miguel (now called Piura), in the far north of Peru, on the border with Ecuador. Pizarro had participated as a captain in the conquest of Central America; he now desperately wanted to conquer lands for himself. When he learned that ships laden with riches had been intercepted while coming up the coast of Ecuador, he immediately understood his new goal. To achieve it, he forged an alliance with Diego de Almagro, who was another ruthless captain, and sailed southward.

Atahuallpa was informed of Pizarro's landing, and using his spies followed the movements of the Spanish through the continent. On his part, Pizarro, knowing that he could not count on surprise, wanted to meet Atahuallpa and offer him his alliance as victor in the civil war that he had learned out

about in talking to local lords. Pizarro clearly hoped to gain advantage from the situation.

The story of these two men's historic encounter in Cajamarca is one of how two worlds, very distant and very different, came to meet and to clash. Only through understanding the difference in the manner and intentions of Atahuallpa and Pizarro can we ever explain how the Spanish captain and his few men managed to capture the Inca, thus rendering useless the huge army that accompanied him and bringing the Tawantinsuyu to a rapid decline that enabled the Spanish to triumphantly enter Cuzco – just one year after the Cajamarca meeting.

But let us see how things unfolded. With the Inca having agreed to receive the new arrivals, and after the exchange of many gifts, Atahuallpa and Pizarro were ready to meet. Thus, the Spanish began their challenging march toward Cajamarca. Upon his arrival in the citadel, Pizarro found it nearly deserted. He immediately ordered his brother Hernando and Captain de Soto to reach Atahuallpa and his army just outside the city to negotiate for a formal encounter. Interpreter Martín and 15 horsemen rode out. In crossing the vast camp with over 20,000 people, as we learn from the chroniclers, the captains soon realized just how many men Atahuallpa could count on.

The imperial court accepted the diplomatic mission coldly, but let the Spanish leave without incident. The meeting was to take place the next day. On the afternoon of November 16th, after what had been a sleepless night for the Spanish, Atahuallpa entered the main square of Cajamarca with a following composed of his leading nobles and about one thousand royal guards. Only Vicente Valverde (the Dominican who was with the *conquistadores*) went to meet them, accompanied by a few armed Spanish. Pizarro, who had only 168 men, had hidden in the city in the meantime, ready to react according to how things went.

As his first gesture Vicente Valverde showed the Bible to Atahuallpa, asking him to embrace the Catholic religion and swear obedience to the kings of Spain. When Atahuallpa, astonished, refused, Valverde gave a signal and an enormous confusion ensued, leading to the downfall of the Incas. The Spanish charged on horseback, coming out of their hiding places, and the cannons were fired. The confusion and terror in the square had dispersed the royal soldiers, unprepared for firearms and scared at the sight of the strange and enormous horses of the Spanish. Many Incas lost their lives, and there was such incredulity at what was going on that the soldiers, unaware of the danger to their sovereign, were busy holding his sedan instead of defending him or trying to carry him away. The effect of surprise and the audacity of the Spanish worked: Atahuallpa fell into the hands of the newcomers.

With an incredible *coup de main*, the Spanish had become the masters of the situation: with the Inca a prisoner, theirs had become a strong position.

Thwarted by knowing that the Inca, the earthly representative of the gods, was in captivity, the Inca lords decided not to count-

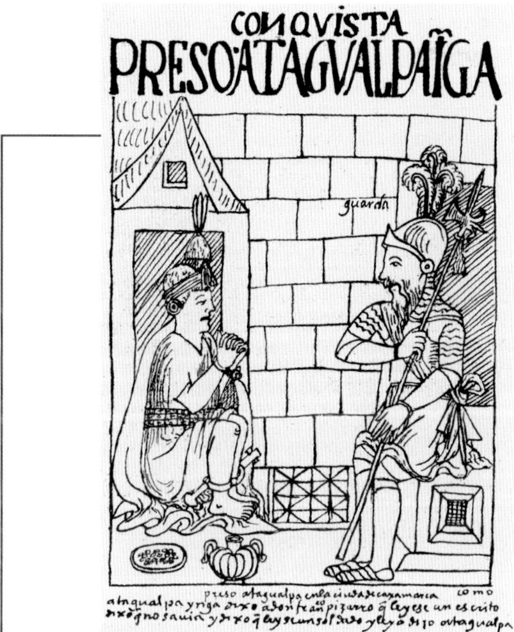

er-attack as long as Atahuallpa was in the hands of Pizarro. Atahuallpa on his part, having quickly understood how greedy the Spanish were, offered them a ransom for his life: if they freed him, he would have given them a room full of gold and silver.

In the following days a great quantity of gold and silver from throughout the empire began to flow into Cajamarca to make up the ransom. In the meantime, Pizarro took advantage of having Atahuallpa prisoner to learn more about the condition of the country and the civil war. But it was not Pizarro's intention that Atahuallpa was to survive his captivity: the situation was becoming too dangerous. If, at the beginning, the Spanish could count on the effects of surprise, they knew that the Incas would recover from the shock and would organize a plan of resistance.

As soon as the *cuarto de rescate* (the "room of the ransom") was full of gold, Francisco Pizarro found an excuse to get rid of his prisoner. Atahuallpa himself provided this involuntarily: in fact, when Pizarro found out that Huascar was a prisoner of Atahuallpa's army, he ordered the sovereign to free him and have him brought to Cajamarca. At that point Atahuallpa feared that Pizarro wanted to make his defeated brother Inca, so as to have an infinitely grateful and malleable puppet. He therefore managed to send a secret message saying that his former rival was to be killed.

In the meantime, Pizarro was joined by reinforcements from Panama, brought by his partner Diego de Almagro (April 1533). On July 26th, 1533, after he had found an excuse to send Hernando de Soto (the only Spaniard with whom Atahuallpa had friendly relations) away from Cajamarca, Pizarro and his men staged a ridiculous trial for Atahuallpa for the murder of Huascar and for treason. They then sentenced Atahuallpa to death. Even though the gold and silver he had secured for them – which was enough to fill a whole room (and increased the greed of the newcomers, who had in the meantime realized the empire's wealth) – Atahuallpa was not capable of saving his own life. At the point of death, he embraced the Catholic religion, and having been baptized, he was allowed to die by strangulation rather than being burned at the stake. This meant that subsequently that his followers were at least able to remove his body from the church in Cajamarca and to hide the mummy on some mountain in the area.

170 - The Inca Atahuallpa's execution took place to avoid the danger of an Inca rebellion (from Theodore de Bry, *Americae*, part VI, 1596).

171 - Atahuallpa spent a long time as prisoner of the Spaniards before being executed in spite of having paid a ransom (from Guaman Poma de Ayala's *Chronicle*).

THE CUARTO DE RESCATE (THE ROOM OF THE RANSOM) AND THE INCA GOLD

Chroniclers tell how 3108 cu. ft (88 cubic m) of gold and silver had been tbrought to Cajamarca to pay the ransom. These precious metals were stored in the room which Atahuallpa had promised to fill to the ceiling to save his life: it was about 20.3 x 15.7 ft (6.2 by 4.8 m). The gold came mainly from the enormous quantity of artifacts which the Incas had to reluctantly take from the temples and from the personal treasure of the sovereign: gold vases weighing up to 51/66 lbs (23/30 kg), gold idols and sheets of gold. It seems obvious that this did no more than increase the Spaniards' greed: among other things, in those months Pizarro had sent two delegations, one to Cuzco and the other to Pachacamac; they reported to him on the great quantity of riches the country had. In his *Primera parte de la crónica del Perú* [1553], the chronicler Cieza de León wrote: "I believe (…) that there is no other realm in the world so rich in metal as every day immense gold and silver veins were discovered, and it such richness could be accumulated and possessed because in many parts of the province gold was gathered from the rivers and silver from the mountains, and all for the king…" (Part II, chapter 14).

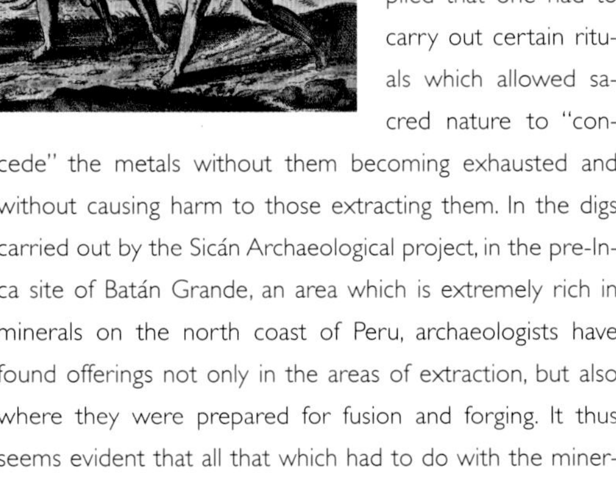

Upon the death of Atahuallpa, and after the so-called royal fifth (i.e., the 20 percent destined for the Spanish king) had been set aside), the gold and silver were melted down to be shared among those who had participated in the Cajamarca enterprise. The rewards for each soldier were enormous, especially for the horsemen who had had played a key role and who had to regain their initial investment in their horses and armor. Pizarro kept a signficant part of the loot for himself and changed his fate forever: he transformed himself from the illegitimate and poor son of a farming woman and a Spanish *hidalgo* to the most powerful man of the Americas, on par with Cortés, the *conquistador* of Mexico, who was of noble origin.

Driven by the will to accumulate riches, the *conquistadors* consigned a whole heritage to be melted down. This had a profound effect on the Inca people: the precious metals were not only a symbol of rank and power but also a direct emanation from the gods. In particular, gold was considered the "sweat" of the sun god, and silver the "tears" of his wife, the moon. This was why the mining of the two metals even before the Inca dominion was an activity strictly regulated by state and local elites. To extract metal, like cultivating the land or rearing animals, was an activity which had to be carried out within a reciprocal rapport with nature: this implied that one had to carry out certain rituals which allowed sacred nature to "concede" the metals without them becoming exhausted and without causing harm to those extracting them. In the digs carried out by the Sicán Archaeological project, in the pre-Inca site of Batán Grande, an area which is extremely rich in minerals on the north coast of Peru, archaeologists have found offerings not only in the areas of extraction, but also where they were prepared for fusion and forging. It thus seems evident that all that which had to do with the minerals had a much higher value than that of prestige.

This vision of the fruition of resources was completely

alien to the newcomer Europeans: once they had finished looting the treasures of the empire, the Spanish did not waste any time and as early as 1545 were systematically exploiting the extremely rich Potosí silver mine in Bolivia. This produced so much wealth that when shipped to Spain it influenced the economic equilibrium within Europe.

The pre-Hispanic people were masters in the working of jewellery: the use of alloys of different metals (such as gold mixed with silver and/or copper, for example) enabled them to obtain a wide range of colors used for matching with other materials. Besides this, the hand-made articles, especially the gold ones, could be covered with vermilion to give the objects red surface veins. The alloys also made the metals more malleable, melting at lower temperatures. Among the most used was the *tumbaga*, a mix of gold and copper: the copper oxides which formed on the surface after the fusion were eliminated with a bath in an acid solution, obtained with from juice of certain plants and urine.

Deposits of metal were abundant throughout the whole country and were relatively accessible, especially those situated in the northern part of the Peruvian Cordillera, from which silver and copper could be extracted. Gold could be collected in nuggets from the riverbeds. In the 16th century, using a metal-working technique that was thousands of years old, the Incas started large-scale processing through work shifts. They also centralized the development of the many metal deposits in the Andes and proclaimed the mines to be the private possession of the sovereigns.

Once the mineral had been extracted and the alloy made, numerous processing techniques were available, from the simplest such as hammering to the more complex with the plating of objects and "lost wax casting." Lost wax casting was a technique in which a wax model of the object which was covered with a layer of clay, leaving two holes respectively at the top and bottom of the model. Then the molten gold was poured into the top hole of the cast, melting the wax, which left from the lower hole. After some cooling, the ceramic mould was broken and the solid gold object cleaned and polished. Many of the fine statuettes representing miniature men and women of the Inca culture were made this way.

During the Inca period the greatest wealth of knowledge about metalworking was that of the Chimú goldsmiths; it was not by chance that they were deported to Cuzco after their homeland was conquered by the Children of the Sun. There they could serve the imperial court. Once the Incas had come in contact with the refined goldsmiths of the northern coast, they absorbed northern traditions and exerted their control on the local production of metal goods.

The Inca artisans produced small items, such as devotional statuettes of llamas, cups, ceremonial arms, war artifacts and *tumi*, or ceremonial knives whose shape was directly taken from Chimú types, *tupus*, i.e., brooches for clothes. They also made bigger things such as large-sized idols and architectural ornaments like the plaques which adorned the walls of the Coricancha of Cuzco, removed very early in the colonial period.

172 - In this engraving by Theodore de Bry (*Americae*, part VI, 1596) the Incas hand over gold to the Spanish as a ransom for Atahuallpa.

173 - Theodore de Bry's illustration (*Americae*, part VI, 1596) shows how metal was forged in an Inca-era manufacturory in Ecuador.

174 - This silver cup is shaped in the form of a man's face (Gold Museum, Lima).

175 left - In the silver cup the figure has bird like features and is wearing a necklace (Musée d'Ethnographie, Geneva).

175 right - The decorative elements of silver cups was often embossed (Musées Royaux d'Art et d'Histoire, Brussels).

176-177 and 178-179 - The group of silver ritual statuettes shows a high level of stylization (Museo de América, Madrid).

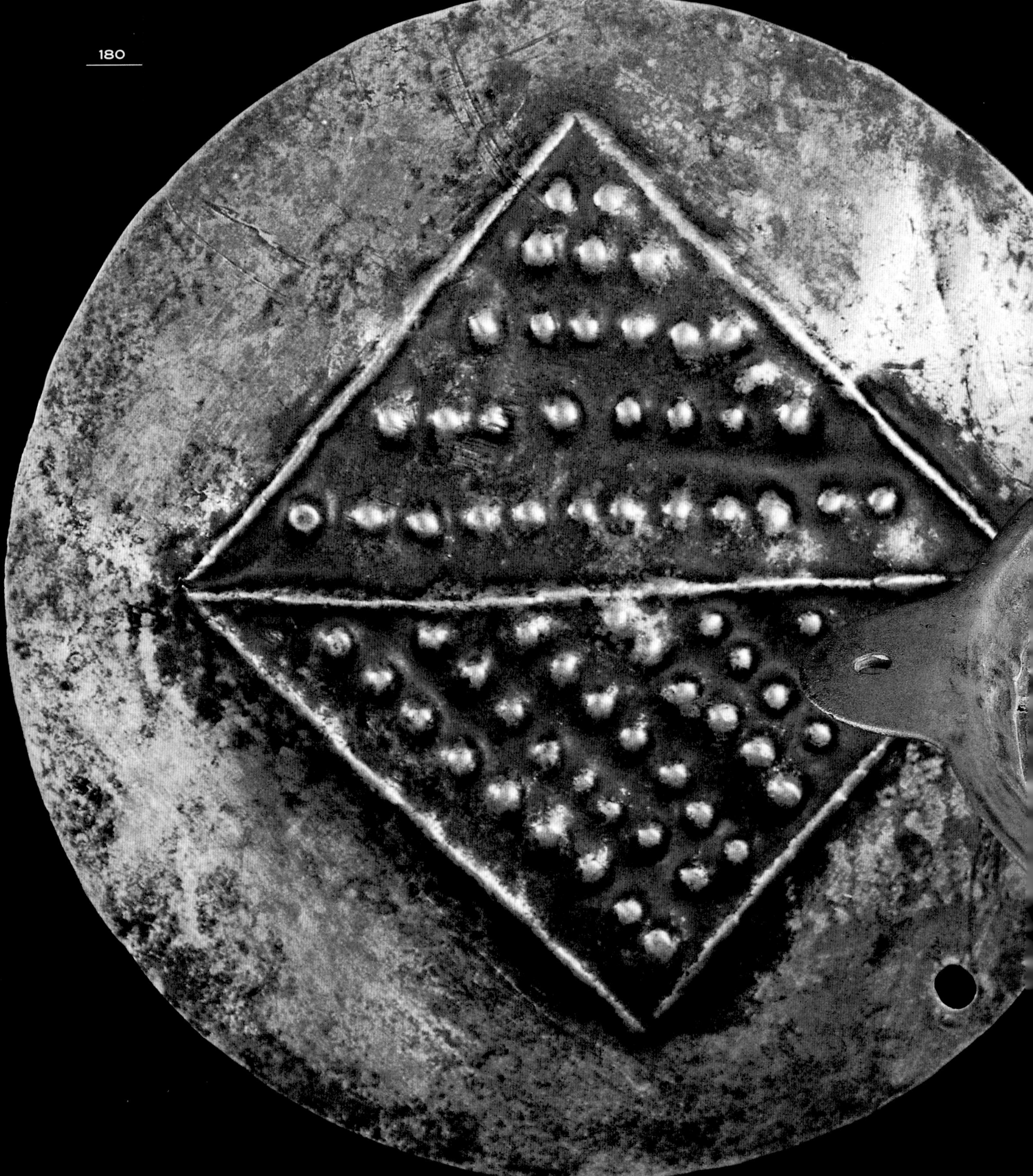

180 - The Inca ornamental and decorative styles are characterized by a strong search for symmetry and for geometric balance in which, as in this silver ornament, the reflection of such Andean values as dualism and bipartition is relevant (Bowers Museum of Cultural Arts, Santa Ana).

181 - This silver and gold washbowl (5.1 inches/13 cm in height) depicts a frieze of men and animals (at the exterior) and a man and a llama in the interior (Inca Museum de la Universidad San Antonio Abad, Cuzco).

182 TOP - THIS GOLD ORNAMENT (14.7 INCHES/37.5 CM LONG) COMES FROM A CHIMÚ TOMB IN THE COASTAL ZONE OF HUARMEY, WHERE A RICH ARRAY OF GRAVE GOODS HAS BEEN FOUND. THE OBJECT IS FORMED BY AN ASSEMBLY OF TUBULAR ELEMENTS WHICH RECALL THE NECKLACES AND PECTORALS OF THE LORD OF SIPÁN'S TREASURE (DUMBARTON OAKS COLLECTION, WASHINGTON, D.C.).

182 BOTTOM - THE GOLD *NARINGUERA* (0.9 INCHES/2.5 CM IN HEIGHT) INLAID WITH LAPIS LAZULI AND SHELLS WAS PROBABLY PART OF THE SAME CHIMÚ GRAVE GOODS ASSEMBLAGE (DUMBARTON OAKS COLLECTION, WASHINGTON, D.C.).

183 - This Chimú gold leather ornament (1.9 inches/5 cm) depicts two figures standing next to each other and some vases. The left part of the ornament is incomplete (Musées Royaux d'Art et d'Histoire, Brussels).

184-185 - This Sicán-Lambayeque gold funerary mask 9.4 inches/24 cm in height) is characterized by the wing-shaped eyes, which allude to the mythological deities of Peru's the north coast (Rautenstrauch-Joest Museum, Cologne).

THE CEREMONIAL CENTER OF PACHACAMAC

Among the first expeditions in Peruvian territory after the Cajamarca events was one undertaken to Pachacamac by Pizarro's brother Hernando. His goal was to pillage the sanctuary, universally recognized as one of the richest in the Andes because of the offerings that were continuously made to this powerful *huaca*. In fact, Pachacamac had remained one of the most visited places of pilgrimage in the Andes since its foundation, ca 2nd century BC, until it was looted and destroyed by the Spanish.

Pachacamac (meaning "Earth-maker" in Quechua) arose on the coast of Peru a few miles south of Lima, on four small promontories near the River Lurín. The temple complex was dedicated to an ancient and important male creator divinity.

The sanctuary grew in importance during the Huari period (from AD 650), when the structures were enlarged. The most important temple built in this phase is now known as the Temple of Pachacamac or the Painted Temple. It is a construction on platforms in adobe (an ancient building tradition on the Peruvian coast), which formed large steps decorated with polychrome paintings. The drawings on the steps, predominantly yellow and pink, took their inspiration from the natural word and were painted with great skill directly on the preparation of the base without leaving additional lines, with brushes made of human hair. Archaeologists have found some of these near the temple.

During the so-called Late Intermediate Period, between AD 1000 and 1450, the sanctuary gained even more importance and new structures were built, in particular the pyramids with its frontal ramps. These were ordered by local rulers in homage to the god Pachacamac. According to recent studies it is also possible that the temples with frontal ramps were not ceremonial complexes but palaces of the lords of the Ychsma ethnic group, who controlled the Lurín Valley at that period, and were transformed into mausoleums by the sovereigns after their deaths.

The Inca were very interested in controlling this *huaca*: when they conquered the coastal area, Pachacamac was absorbed in the official cult of the empire, though without losing its autonomy. This also had happened at Tiwanaku, another Andean religious site, where just as at Pachacamac the Incas ensured that the vital structures remained intact and that new temples were built for the veneration of their official gods. Thus a temple dedicated to the sun (Inti) was built, and a House of Virgins, or Acllahuasi. The imposing

Temple of the Sun was built on the highest rocky promontory of Pachacamac, from where one could enjoy an excellent view over the Pacific Ocean. The total height was about 65 ft (20 m), and the peak has a series of enclosures for the cult. The Acllahuasi was where the virgins dedicated to the care of the temples were housed: these women also prepared the fabrics which were then offered to the divinity. The Pachacamac Acllahuasi is a structure conceived in classic imperial Inca style with a series of cells which open onto a central patio. The central patio is surrounded by trapezoidal niches with double jambs.

On January 30th, 1533, Hernando Pizarro and his men entered Pachacamac. Pizarro knew that much gold was hid-

den in the temple, and he had managed to get the natives to spontaneously offer him some of it to him. Of course, the *conquistador* deemed the amount to be insufficient. In fact, it seems that the priests and native population, fearing pillage, had already removed and hidden much of the gold. Hernando ordered the destruction of the temple and its numerous wooden idols, which were replicas of the main divinity. He was thus the only European to see such an important *huaca* intact. In the following years the Spanish carried out extensive excavations in the ruined temple grounds in search of precious metals; they found and looted gold of Pachacamac. Thus began the ransacking of the coastal area of Peru; it still goes on today.

186 - Pachacamac's Acllahuasi is designed in the classical imperial Inca style.

186-187 - Pachacamac, meaning "Earth-maker" in the Quechua language, was dedicated to an ancient and important male creator deity.

187 - This male statuette bound in fabric and decorated with feathers was offered to Pachacamac (Pachacamac Museum).

THE LAST PHASES OF THE EMPIRE'S EXISTENCE

In the years following their landing of 1532, the Spanish managed to gain control of the entire region. Having soon realized the situation of the country and the tight control which the Inca had exerted on the local *curacas*, Pizarro used his fine diplomatic skills to obtain a series of favors from the heads of local ethnic groups. He presented himself as their liberator from Inca domination. Obviously, at first none of them realized that they were simply going from one situation of being subjects to another which was to prove much heavier and more oppressive. Through this role of liberator, Pizarro managed, just one year after the Cajamarca events, to march southward and in a series of battles defeat what was left of the Inca army. Thus he entered the heart of the Andes world: Cuzco.

After the death of Atahuallpa, Pizarro found it necessary to put a native on the throne, choosing a member of Huascar's family. The man died soon after, but another relative had escaped the massacre by Atahuallpa's generals: Manco Inca. The Spanish, upon reaching Cuzco, hurriedly crowned him in the presence of the mummies of his predecessors. The indigenous rite lasted more than a month: from that time an improbable phase of Inca-Spanish co-government began.

The road ahead of Pizarro was in fact rather steep. Not only were some of Atahuallpa's dangerous generals still alive, continuing to occupy Ecuadorian territory, but Manco Inca became impatient with the Spanish interference in his "government" of the Empire of the Four Parts Together.

Manco realized that by staying in Cuzco he reduced his authority to a mere façade, and so organized an ill-fated escape attempt. He did manage to escape at a later stage and organized an enormous army, which then besieged Cuzco, where a few hundred Spanish had barricaded themselves. Even though the Incas flooded the city to expel the invaders, the Spanish resisted in the Sacsahuaman area, holding out until the Inca army dwindled because of the agricultural cycle: the farmer-soldiers had to go back to their fields and the siege was lifted. At the same time the Incas besieged the new capital founded by the Spanish on the coast. This capital was Ciudad de los Reyes (now Lima), a strategic port from which the Spanish controlled the flow of goods to Europe. As with the siege of Cuzco, the siege of this city failed.

Manco Inca then decided to withdraw to the Vilcabamba area, east of Cuzco, an area of dense and inaccessible wilderness. Here he founded an independent neo-Inca state, which was upheld by his successors after his death, first by Tito Cusi and then by the last Inca, Tupac Amaru.

For thirty years the last Incas tried to re-establish power over their homeland, but in vain. The situation was by then radically changed: what remained of the population, decimated by famine and the diseases brought by the invaders, was rapidly adapting to the new colonial institutions. Also, at least formally, some began to embrace the customs and the new religion imposed by the *conquistadores*: Christianity. The cities changed quickly, and the churches, together with the colonial government palaces, became the fulcrum of the new social life of the Andean area. In Cuzco the Convent of San Domingo was built on top of the Sacred Temple of Coricancha, of which only a part of the spectacular circular wall is still visible today. In contrast, the cathedral was built near the city's central space, formed by the twin squares of Aucaipata and Cusipata, also a very important area during the Inca period. It was the place of ceremonial buildings and from where one watched the most important public celebrations during the empire.

Excluding Cuzco, where Pizarro and his men established themselves in order to control the royal throne in the early phases of the conquest, the new colonial foundations were normally cities set in more accessible areas.

188 - The painting depicts Tupac Amaru, the last Inca ruler. Western portraiture canons mix with the wish to show elements of the native world such as the *tocapu* on the ruler's tunic (Museo Nacional de Historia, Lima).

The men of the Cajamarca encounter first took upon themselves the government of the best terrain in the empire. The Spanish became *encomenderos*, i.e., men in the service of the crown, charged with the task of keeping to order on the lands, christianizing the natives and, in theory, ensuring their state of good health so as that could be productive and pay taxes. But during the viceroyalty that followed the first phase of the conquest (when the Spanish crown sent a series of governors to the Peruvian territory to rule the country), corruption was rife. Not only among the Spanish, who dramatically exploited to local population, but also among the ethnic chiefs who had been promised advantages in exchange for their allegiance. In fact, by order of Emperor Charles V the first viceroy, Blasco Nuñez Vela (1490-1546), uprooted the *encomiendas* from the territory.

After that, during the viceroyalty of Francisco de Toledo (1569-1581), sent to impose better government over the indigenous population, a system of *reducciones* was set up, i.e., forced relocations. People had to leave their settlements (typically in very high and easily defendable areas) to go and live in the new cities or production centers, the *obraje*.

These systematic deportations, like those that the Incas had enforced at the time of their conquests, was aimed at concentrating the workforce in easily controllable areas, but it also removed the people from their indigenous roots. Thus they lost the protection of their gods, who lived in the mountains or grottoes, and their sense of ethnic belonging. In this manner their will to defend their way of life, which was rooted in the care and love of their land of origin, was diminished. So, notwithstanding that the Incas of Vilcabamba were fomenting some localized rebellion, they could no longer count on the organization of the state machine based on the two-way communication between the Inca and local ethnicities. Now the *curacas* no longer dealt with the administrators of Tawantinsuyu, but with the Spanish to whom they had to subject themselves to survive.

Now isolated, the Vilcabambas Incas were defeated by a powerful expedition ordered sent by Viceroy Toledo into their forest retreats. In 1572, Tupac Amaru was captured and put to death in Cuzco in 1572.

After the execution of the formal leader of the resistance, the neo-Inca movements survived in the form of clandestine indigenous cults in the *huacas*, and in the so-called *taki onqoy*: a movement born in Huamanga, in the central-northern *sierra* of Peru around 1560. From there it extended to Lima, to Cuzco and to Bolivia. *Taki onqoy* means "dance disease": those involved believed that the *huacas*, the old pre-Hispanic divinities, took possession of the bodies of the indigenous inhabitants and made them dance and sing until they collapsed, demonstrating their opposition to the spread of Christianity. Changing from a rebellious movement to a religious one, *taki onqoy* soon became a political movement. It was discovered and disbanded after one of its members revealed its existence during his confession of sins.

Taki onqoy nonetheless remained a symbol of the Incas' will for independence, as did the other indigenous movements of the first colonial period that tell of the hostility to the Spanish born of the indigenous peoples' belief in their local divinities. Such movements are part of the mythical tales that can still be heard today, passed on from father to son over the centuries in the native language.

189 - With the arrival of the Spaniards, native artistic production became enriched with new techniques such as painting on canvas. In this scene an Inca princess beheads an enemy (Inca Museum de la Universidad San Antonio Abad, Cuzco).

190 - A year after the encounter of Cajamarca, Spanish soldiers enter Cuzco (from Theodore de Bry, *Americae*, part VI, 1596).

190-191 - The Spaniards fight against the Incas below the walls of Cuzco (from Theodore de Bry, *Americae*, part VI, 1596).

192-193 - During the Spaniards' advance, they suppressed the fires of rebellion in a violent way: however, conscious of their numerical inferiority, the Spaniards tried to form alliances with the local ethnic leaders, seeking to appeal to their hope of relief from the Inca dominion (from Theodore de Bry, *Americae*, part VI, 1596).

193 - The Spaniards forced newly conquered peoples to perform obligatory labor on the land. After a temporary confusion, the Inca resistance reorganized itself, using war tactics aimed to neutralize the technological superiority of European weapons (from Theodore de Bry, *Americae*, part VI, 1596).

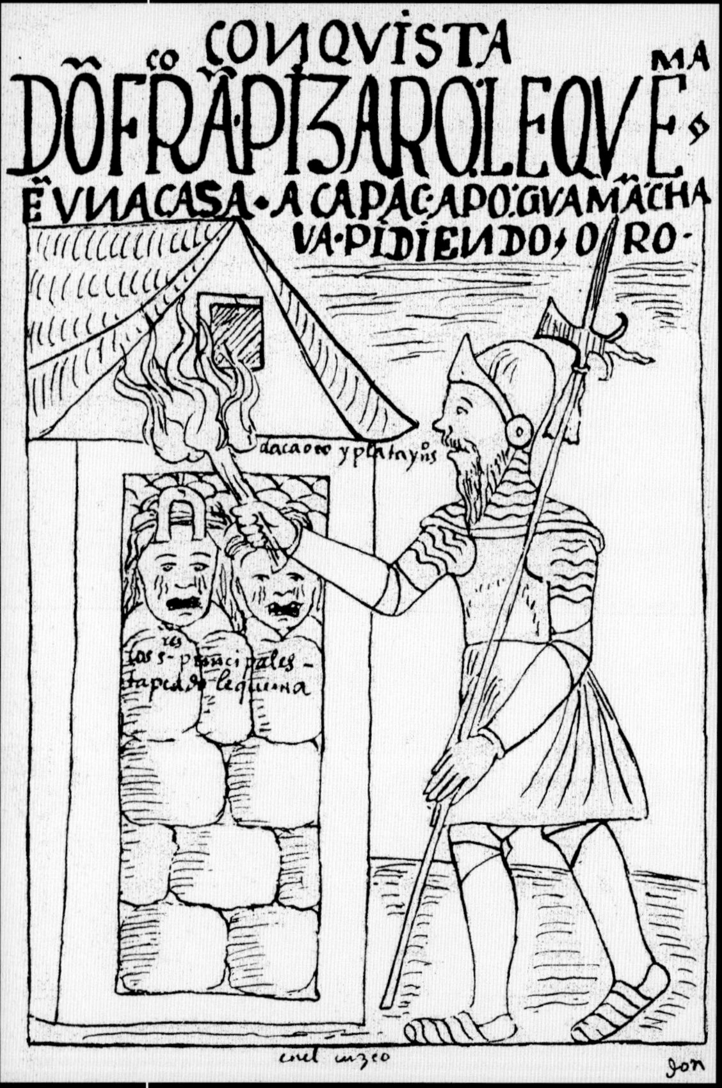

194 left - The Spaniards plundered as much gold as possible. In this scene Pizarro sets fire to an Inca nobleman's house

194 right - Dissension among the Spaniards favored the native resistance: a powerful *curaca* captures Francisco Hernández Girón

195 - The last Incas took cover in the forests creating an independent realm in an isolated region. For several years sovereign, Tupac Amaru, was captured and dragged to Cuzco by the Spanish captain Martín Garcia de Loyola. The Inca was then

THE ORGANIZATION OF THE INCA ARMY AND WAR TACTICS

The organization of the Inca army created great interest among the Spaniards: the soldier-chroniclers of the first period immediately tried to understand their enemy's tactics, how they were structured into military levels and what logistical facilities there were in support of the army. The reports of immense armies were naturally part of European propaganda aimed at giving an aura of epic enterprise to the advance of the *conquistadores* on the Peruvian territory. However, it is true that the Inca first managed to organize a great army thanks to the system of work shifts (*mita*). The Inca himself led the army; his role as a charismatic leader was fundamental to encouraging the soldiers. However, though the sovereign had a first-person role in the first phase of the expansion of the empire, we see that the kings progressively transferred command of their troops to their family members (for instance to a brother) or to their young sons who, as princes, had to demonstrate their skills in war. But in case of extreme necessity, the sovereign's descent into battle had a very important effect on the army's morale: we saw that in the civil war between Atahuallpa and Huascar both sovereigns tried to ensure a decisive battle by personally leading their armies.

The sovereign would reach the battlefield on a sedan, symbol of his rank and surrounded by his personal guard: to overturn the sedan and capture or kill the Inca meant ending the conflict. In the same manner, the Inca rulers tried to defeat their enemies by capturing their charismatic leaders dead or alive (we know in fact that it was a custom among Inca rulers to bring the mummies of their ancestors onto the battlefield) if they were fortunate enough to identify them.

Immediately under the Inca there were at least two generals in charge (as with other aspects of Inca society, the army was organized according to a dual system). The general commanded battalions made up of units of men (10, 100, 1000 and 10000), according to a decimal division which reflected that generally used for the census of the population and for tax collections. These battalions were led by ethnic chiefs who led soldiers from their own groups into battle.

Even in the army there were specialized roles that were carried out by specific people; for example, after they had been conquered, the Chachapoyas and Cañars were often enrolled in the Inca's personal guard, even though traditionally this special corps was made up of young noblemen from Cuzco who had received special military training.

The auqa camayoc (soldiers) were married men between 25 and 50 years old. They were not in permanent service with the army but dedicated a shift of their *mita* on a rotation system. During campaigns the soldiers' wives, relatives and even young children often accompanied them. This meant that the army advanced with an incredible number of people, of whom only a part had any military role. There were also support groups, such as carriers, messengers, scouts and so on.

The armies' logistical support structures grew as the expansion of the Inca became supra-regional. The short skirmishes that occurred early in the Inca dominion did not require extensive logistics, and only when war became an important matter for the empire did the Incas begin to built fortresses in strategic areas, in particular in that of northern Bolivia and troubled Ecuador. Here conquests were less solid. Paradoxically we find few fortifications along the external borders of the empire, a sign that it was considered more urgent to pacify internal revolts than to face enemies from outside. Furthermore, as we have already hinted, Tawantinsuyu did not have a territorial continuity with borders like a modern national state but was rather an agglomeration of territories of different ethnicities that made up the Inca domain.

Although the Inca ruler could count on an army that during such campaigns as Manco Capac's siege of Cuzco reached 100,000 men, the Incas were defenseless against the Spaniards. It is clear that the Europeans could count on the technological advantage of firearms and horses, even though the Inca soon learnt to avoid facing their enemy in open fields (where the Spaniards could use cavalry and firearms most effectively). They opted for man-to-man fighting in the most impervious areas, where the Spaniards had a harder time. Pizarro's men were mercenaries, ready for anything, and most had had 20 years' experience of warfare in the New World. Thus they managed to make the most of the native peoples' initial discouragement and turn it into an advantage as reinforcements arrived for future invasions.

197 left - The Inca Huayna Capac is depicted leading a battle while is carried on a war litter (from Guamán Poma de Ayala's *Chronicle*).

197 top right - Challcochima was a worthy leader of the Inca army.

197 bottom right - Incas demonstrate their fighting abilities when young.

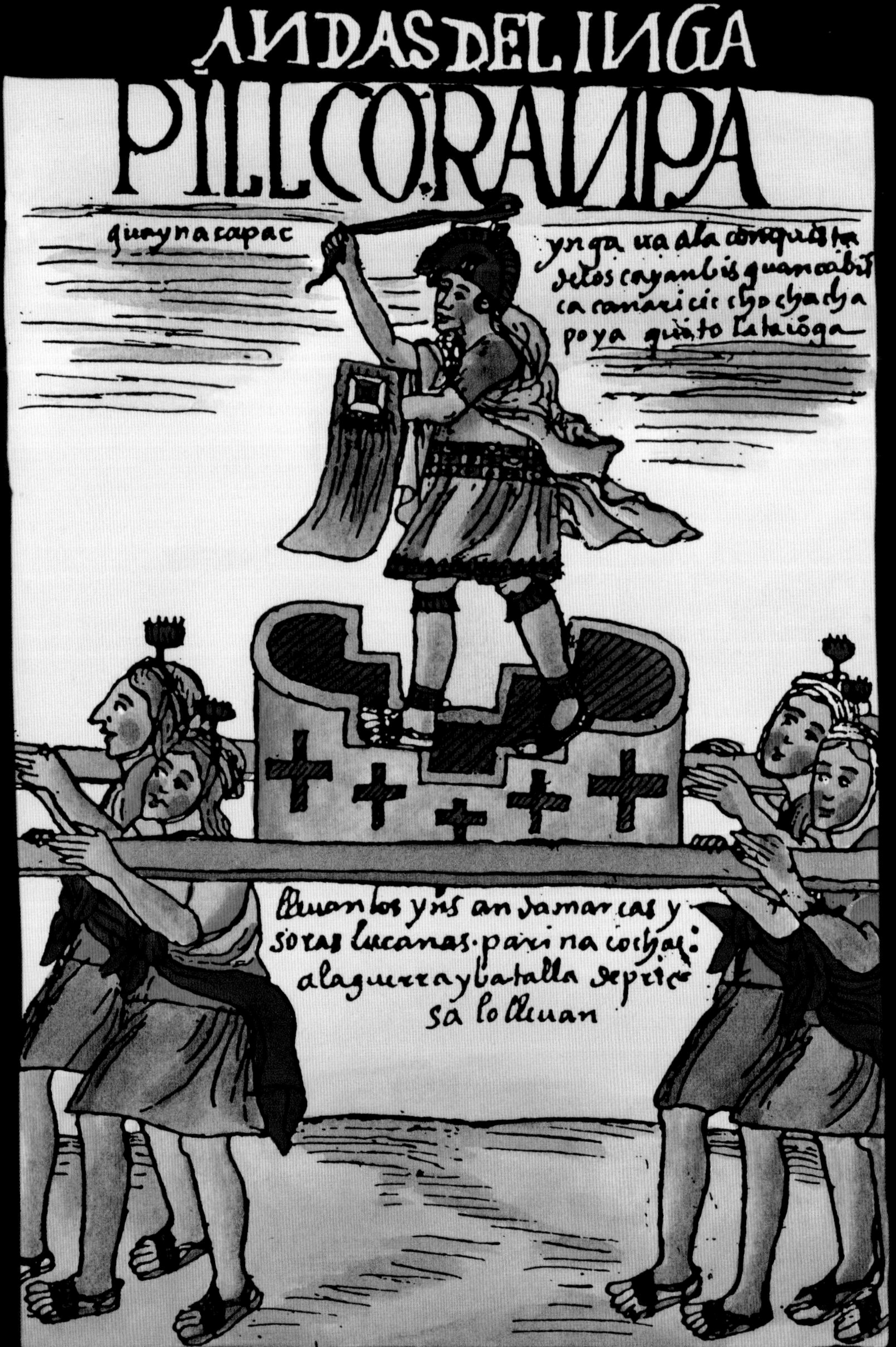

ANDAS DEL INGA

PILLCO.RANPA

guayna capac

ynga ua ala conquista delos cayanbis guancabilca cañari cic cho chacha poya quito lataconga

lleuan los yns andamarcas y soras lucanas. pari na cochas: ala guerra y batalla de pricsa lo lleuan

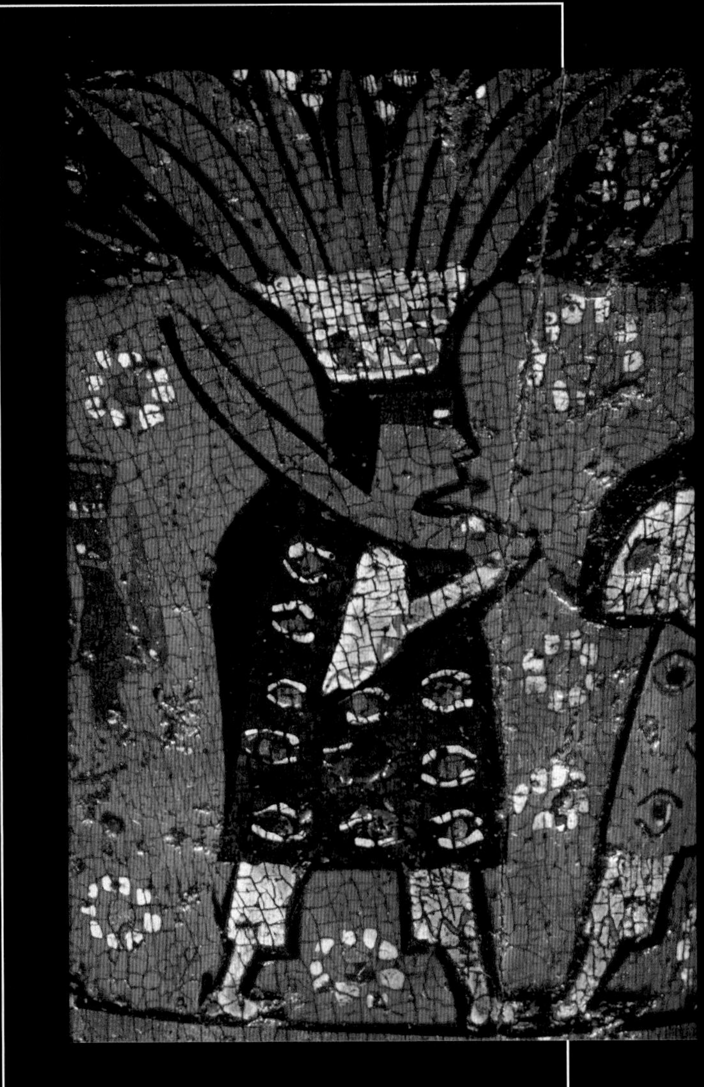

198 - This detail of an Inca *quero* (dating to the 15th-16th centuries) depicts a figure with an armed profile and with an enormous feather headdress (Inca Museum de la Universidad San Antonio Abad, Cuzco).

199 - Wooden *queros* were often painted with scenes that recalled the mythical and religious world of the Children of the Sun. In this case a nobleman is depicted during a battle scene (Inca Museum de la Universidad San Antonio Abad, Cuzco).

THE INCA HERITAGE

The discovery of the Americas sparked an unprecedented debate in 16th-century Europe, which led to review of the hitherto generally accepted paradigms and to a new type of reflection on the matter of relations with "the other." This reflection – or rethinking – has not yet ended. This new intellectual opportunity was also accompanied by the possibility of securing products which were to change the habits of Europe: many goods in common use, such as coffee, cocoa, chili pepper, and tobacco among other things, came to Europe from America.

The most important Andean contribution to European agriculture was the potato, whose role in the feeding the Old Continent was very significant; it was immediately introduced to the areas of northern Europe, where the climate was colder and the risk of famine higher than in the south. The Andean tuber became so fundamental in feeding the European population that when a fungus struck Ireland's potato harvest, destroying nearly a third of the crop in 1845 and the whole crop in 1846 and again in 1848, it caused a terrible famine which forced many Irishmen to emigrate to the United States. Also noteworthy was the discovery and development by the Spanish of the Cerro Rico mine ("Rich Mountain") of Potosí, in Bolivia. Silver was extracted from ore thanks to the skills of the Indios, assigned to work by the *mita* system. After the first few years of modest efficiency, the Spanish secured greater rewards by managing to extract the silver from the ore by means of an amalgam of the latter with mercury, which was extracted in the Santa Barbara mines in Peru. The result was that Potosí became the most productive silver mine of its time, and the city the most populous in the Americas, after Mexico City. But this wealth came with a terrible death rate among indigenous miners because of appalling working conditions and the deadly fumes from the mercury. The situation reached a point that one could calculate how many Indians were dying per kilo of silver extracted. In addition, the value of silver dropped sharply in Europe because of the quantity available, and it brought an inflation rate which nearly collapsed the economy. The innovations introduced during centuries of change in the pre-Hispanic period, which culminated in the organization of a great empire during Inca times, are still at the core of some social institutions and uses in the rural areas of the Andes. In many communities there is still collective work (the *faenas*), the sacred landscape of the Andes is still venerated and a cult of the dead still continues, even though in the new forms that the ever-changing Andean society has created. These patterns have a very strong bond with the past. The main languages of the Inca Empire were Quechua and Aymara, used by evangelizers as languages in which to teach the gospel to a population which spoke uncounted dialects, and the two languages are still the most widespread in the Andean area. But what perhaps is more revealing is that the Inca Empire, as a unifying event (though with the limitations which we saw) in the history of the pre-Hispanic Andes, has remained in the popular imagination as the strongest symbol of cultural belonging. For this reason one is not surprised by how the mythical history of the

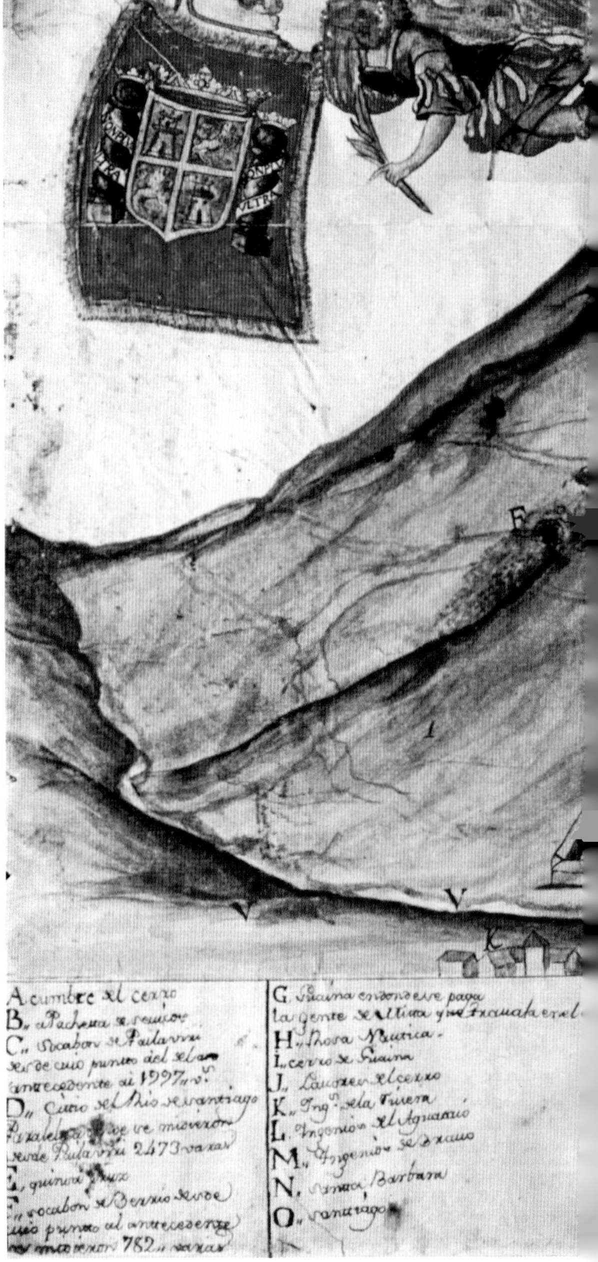

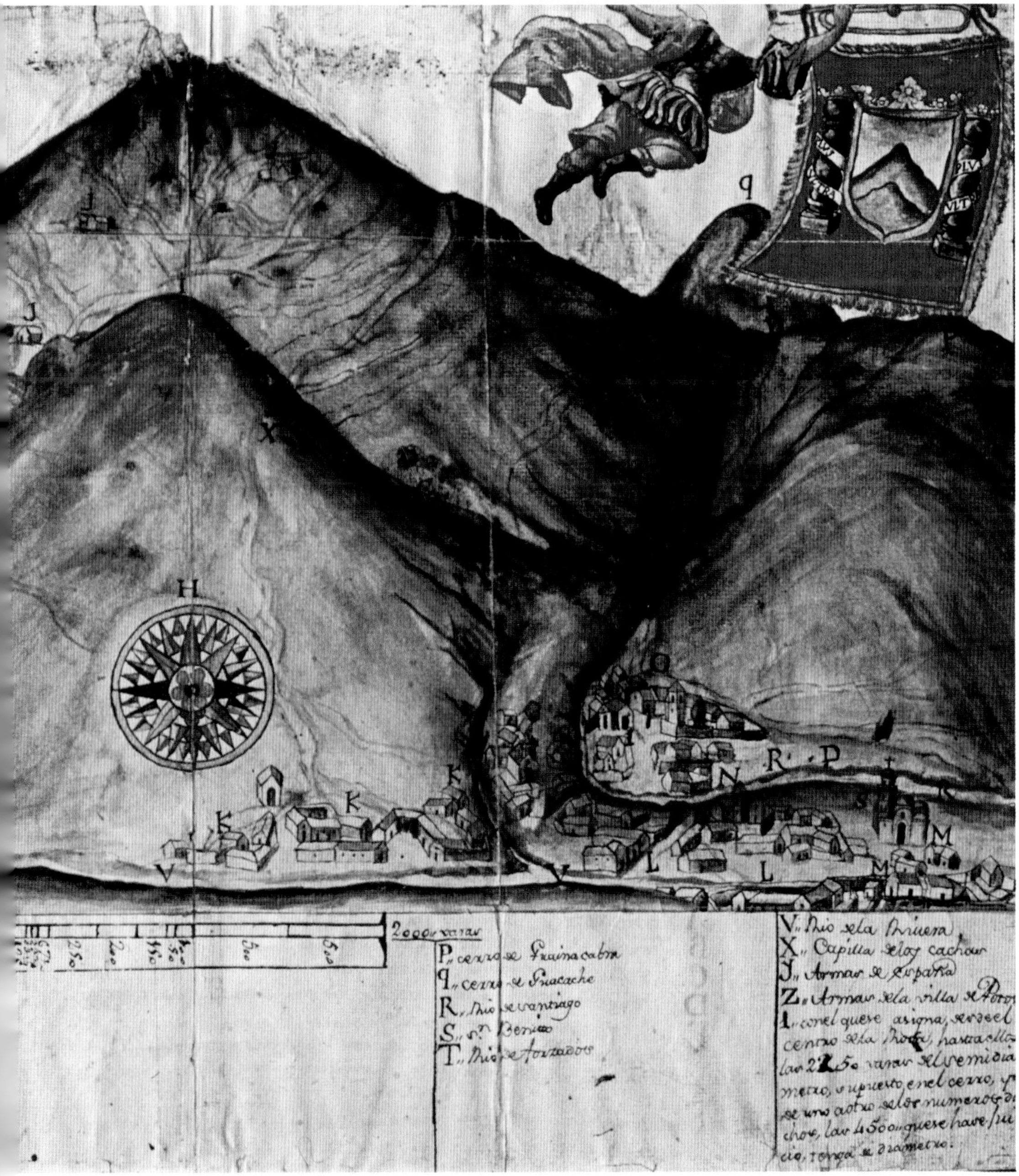

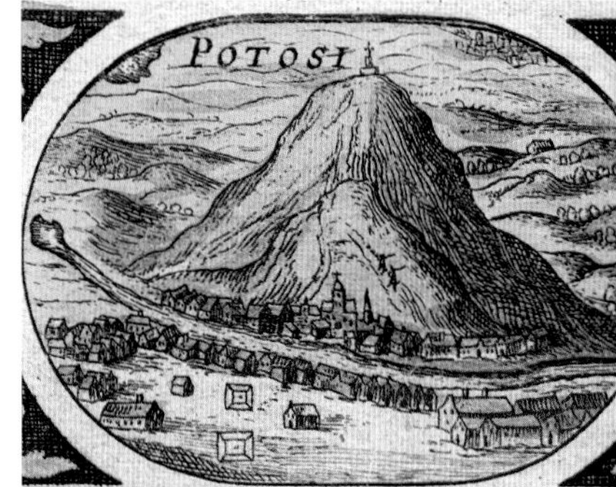

Incas has often been used as a means of propaganda by the independence movements against the Spanish government, firstly in the rebellion led by Tupac Amaru II in 1780, and more recently by modern indigenous movements. The myth which the Incas built on their unified magical and divine history that in turn had been necessary to justify their rise to power has now become the banner of modern Andean nations.

200-201 AND 201 - THE EXPLOITATION OF THE CERRO RICO OF POTOSÍ IN BOLIVIA REVOLUTIONIZED THE EUROPEAN ECONOMY BECAUSE OF THE ENORMOUS QUANTITY OF PRECIOUS METAL WHICH THE SPANISH BROUGHT INTO THE MARKETS. THE SMALL VILLAGE AT THE FOOT OF THE MOUNTAINS QUICKLY BECAME ONE OF AMERICA'S LARGEST SETTLEMENTS.

A
C
B
F
D
A.... Sra Prinsipal con sunegra,
Esclava
....Arbol de Granadillas, y su Fruta.
....Arbol del Nispero, y su Fruta.
....Fruta con nombre de Narangillas.
....Palma de Cocos grandes.
....Arbol de Coquitos de chile.
Visente Alban, pintor en
Quito, à. 1783.
2

202 - The conquest of the Americas brought to Europe new plants and fruits which were systematically represented in the paintings of the 17th and 18th centuries. A noblewoman of Quito is portrayed accompanied by a slave (Vicente Albán, 1783; Museo de América, Madrid).

203 - In addition to the new class of governors imposed by the conquest, portraits of native men, like this one of Yumbo ethnicity, are common in the series of paintings which depict the New World. This scene is from the Quito region of Ecuador (Vicente Albán, 1783; Museo de América, Madrid).

AUTHOR

Carolina Orsini (1972) is curator of the Extra-European Collections of the City Collections of Applied Arts of the Castello Sforzesco, Milan. For nearly a decade she has undertaken – and still undertakes – field work in the Peruvian Andes, where she directs the works of the Antonio Raimondi Archaeology and Anthropology Mission, in collaboration with the Italian Ministry of Foreign Affairs and various Peruvian institutions. Orsini graduated in Indigenous Civilizations of America at the University of Bologna; she obtained a diploma in archaeology at the High School for Cultural Heritage of the Scuola Normale Superiore of Pisa and she subsequently obtained her Ph.D. at the University of Bologna with a thesis on the landscape archaeology of the Chacas Valley in Peru. She is a member of the national board of the Peruvian archaeologists and is one of the Italian representatives for the Corpus Americanensium Italicum project of Brussels' Academy of Sciences. In recent years she has collaborated with many Italian and foreign museums as guest researcher and as scientific consultant for American-themed exhibitions, and has organized various exhibitions on non-European cultures at the Castello Sforzesco. Orsini has written many scientific articles about American-Indian cultures, besides numerous monographs on the ancient pre-Hispanic cultures of Peru.

GLOSSARY

Ayllu: The basic social unit of Andean societies. Based on family groups, it served many sociopolitical and economic functions.

Ceques Lines: Imaginary lines which began at Cuzco and had, as their final point, important places (or *huacas*) which were located in the territory surrounding the capital. Cuzco was thus joined to a network of sacred places directly connected to the heart of the cult: the Coricancha temple.

Curacas: Leaders of the various ethnic groups with which the Incas came into contact during their wars of conquest.

Huacas: The "sacred things." This term refers to temple structures and also to objects that were particularly important or magical. It can also refer to natural locations of a special or sacred nature.

Mita: Mandatory public service in the form of labor which each adult had to undertake for the maintenance of public structures or for the cultivation of communal fields or those whose harvest was destined to the Inca.

Pacarina: Mythical place of origin. Normally it refers to remarkable landmarks, like a particular lagoon, cave or mountain.

Panacas: Cuzco's noble families, based on lineage. Every Inca had the right to form his own *panaca* which became a sort of political organization that sustained the rights of the Inca's family.

Quechua: the term today refers to one of Peru's native languages. The Incas called their own ethnic group's language *runa simi*. They Incas used the term *quechua* to refer to an ecosystem within their territory's Andean range that was the most populated area at the time of the Inca conquest. This meaning is still valid today; Quechua is spoken in the Andes.

Quipu: A system of small knotted ropes that dangled from a main rope. The *quipus* were used to record numerical data and information.

Tawantinsuyu: "The Four Parts Together"; the term the Incas used to define their territory, which was formed by four large "regions."

BIBLIOGRAPHY

Ancient Sources

BETANZOS J. DE, 1968 [1551], *Suma y narracíon de los Incas*, Biblioteca de Autores Españoles, Tomo CCIX, Madrid.
CIEZA DE LEÓN P., 1984 [1553], *Primera parte de la crónica del Perú*,, Ed. M. Ballesteros, Historia 16, Madrid.
COBO B., 1956 [1653], *Historia de Nuevo Mundo*, Biblioteca de Autores Españoles, Obras del P. Bernabé Cobo, Madrid, Tomos LXXXXI, LXXXII.
GARCILASO DE LA VEGA, EL INCA, 1977 [1609], *Primera parte de los Commentarios Reales que tratan del origen de los Yncas, Reyes que fueron del Peru* [...], Italian edition, F. Saba Sardi, Rusconi, Milan.
GUAMAN POMA DE AYALA F., 1987 [1613-15], *Nueva corónica i buen gobierno*, Ed. J.V. Murra, R. Adorno, J. L. Urioste, 3 vols. Historia 16, Madrid.
POLO DE ONDEGARDO J., 1916 [1571], *Informaciones acerca de la Religión y Gobierno de los Incas*. Libros y Documentos referentes a la historia del Perú, Coleccion de Vargas Ugarte, Lima.
SANCHO DE LA HOZ P., 1987 [1534], *Cartas y cronistas del descubrimiento y la conquista*, Edicciones Horizonte, Lima.
SARMIENTO DE GAMBOA P., 1969 [1572], *Historia de los Incas*, in *Obras Completas* del Inca Garcilaso de la Vega, Biblioteca de Autores Españoles, Madrid 1960, tomo IV.

Modern Sources

AGURTO CALVO S., 1987, *Estudios acerca de la construcción, arquitectura y planeamiento Incas*, Cámara Peruana de la Construcción, Lima.
ANGLES VARGAS V., 1970, *P'isaq: Metrópoli Inka*, Industrial Gráfica, Lima.
ASCHER M. - ASCHER R., 1981, *Code of the Quipu: A study in media, mathematics, and culture*, The University of Michigan Press, Ann Arbor.
BINGHAM H., 1913, *In the Wonderland of Peru*, National Geographic Magazine, April 1913.
BAUER B., 1999, *Las antiguas tradiciones alfareras del Cuzco*, Editorial Centro Bartolomé de Las Casas, Cusco.
BAUER B., 2004, *Ancient Cuzco, Heartland of the Inca*, University of Texas Press, Austin.
BONAVIA D., 2004, *Chimú*, in *Americhe e Oceania* (ed. Marco Curatola). Rome, Istituto della Enciclopedia Italiana.
COCK G. A., 2002, *Inca Rescue*, National Geographic Magazine, May 2002.
CURATOLA M., 1992, *Il paese degli inca: da "Regno dell'oro" a "Repubblica" degli Indios*, in PURIN S. (ed.), *Inca Perù*, Leonardo de Luca Editor, Rome.
D'ALTROY T., 2002, *The Incas*, Blackwell Publishers, Oxford.
DUVIOLS P., 1980, *Algunas reflexiones acerca de la tesis de la estructura dual del poder incaico*, Histórica, vol. 9, n. 2, PUCP, Lima.
GASPARINI G. AND MARGOLIES L., 1977, *Arquitectura Inka*, Centro de Investigaciones Históricas y Estéticas, Universidad Central de Venezuela, Caracas.
GAVAZZI A., 2006, *Architettura Inca*, in ORSINI C., *Arte inca*, Collana "La grande storia dell'arte del Sole 24 ore", series, Silvana Editoriale, Cinisello Balsamo.
HYSLOP J., 1984, *The Inka Road System*, Academic Press, New York.
HYSLOP J., 1990, *Inka Settlement Planning*, University of Texas Press, Austin.
ISBELL W.H. AND MCEWAN, G.F. (EDS.), 1991, *Huari Administrative Structure: Prehistoric Monumental Architecture and State Government*, Dumbarton Oaks Research Library and Collection, Washington.
JULIEN J., 2004, *Inca*. In *Americhe e Oceania* (ed. Marco Curatola). Rome, Istituto della Enciclopedia Italiana.
LIVI BACCI M., 2005, *Conquista*, Il Mulino, Bologna.
MC EWAN G. (ED.), 2005, *Pikillacta. The wari Empire in Cuzco*, University of Iowa Press, Iowa City
MURRA J., 1980, *Formazioni economiche e politiche nel mondo andino: saggi di etnostoria*, Einaudi, Turin.
PEASE F., 1978, *Del Tahuantinsuyo a la Historia del Perú*, IEP, Lima.
PEASE F. AND OTHERS, 1999, *Los Incas: Arte y Símbolos*, Colección Arte y Tesoros del Perú, Banco de Crédito del Perú, Lima.
PROTZEN J.P., 1993, *Inca Architecture and Construction at Ollantaytambo*, Oxford University Press, Oxford, New York.
PURIN S. (ED.), 1992, *Inca Perù*, Leonardo de Luca Publishers, Rome.
RAVINES R., 1996, *Pachacamac, Santuario Universal*, Lima, Editorial Los Pinos.
ROSTWOROWSKI M., 1999, *History of the Inca Realm*, Cambridge University Press, Cambridge.
ROWE J.H., 1963, *Urban Settlement in Ancient Peru*, Ñawpa Pacha, n. 1, Berkeley, California.
ROWE J.H., 1967, *What kind of city was Inca Cuzco?*, Ñawpa Pacha, n.5, Berkeley, California.
SANTILLANA J., 2001, *Las plazas del Cusco y el espacio ceremonial inca*, In Los Dioses del antiguo Perú (ed. Makowski K.- Rucabado J.). Lima, Banco de Crédito Lima.
SANTILLANA J., 2004, *Tomebamba*. In *Americhe e Oceania* (ed. Marco Curatola). Rome, Istituto della Enciclopedia Italiana.
TOPIC J., 2004, *Viracochapampa*, in *Enciclopedia Archeologia. Americhe-Oceania*. Istituto della Enciclopedia Italiana. Rome, p. 847.

URTON G. AND AVENI A., 1983, *Archeoastronomical fieldwork on the coast of Peru*, in AVENI A. AND BROTHERSTOM G., *Calendars in Mesoamerica and Peru- Native American computation of time*, BAR international series 174, Oxford.
VENTUROLI S., 2005, *Il paesaggio come testo. La costruzione di un'identità tra territorio e memoria nell'area andina*, Clueb, Bologna.
VILLACORTA L. F., VETTER L., AUSEJO C. (EDS.), 2004, *Puruchuco y la Sociedad de Lima, un Homenaje a Arturo Jiménez Borja*, CONCYTEC / Compañía de Minas Buenaventura / Diagnósticos Gammagráficos, Lima.
WILLIAMS P.R., ISLA J., Nash D., 2001, *Cerro Baúl: un Enclave Wari en Interacción con Tiwanaku*, Boletin de Arqueologia PUCP, Lima, n. 5.
ZUIDEMA T., 1971, *Etnologia e storia. Cuzco e le strutture dell'impero Inca*, Einaudi, Turin.
ZUIDEMA T., 1986, *La civilisation inca au Cusco, (Essais et conférences)*, Presses Universitaires de France, Paris.
ZUIDEMA T., 1990, *Inca Civilization in Cuzco*, University Press of Texas, Austin.

INDEX

c = caption

PHOTOGRAPHIC CREDITS

Page 1 Justin Kerr
Pages 2-3 Antonio Attini/Archivio White Star
Pages 4-5 Massimo Borchi/Archivio White Star
Page 6 Gianni Dagli Orti/Corbis
Page 8 Raphael Gaillarde/Gamma/Contrasto
Page 9 Aisa
Page 11 Photoservice Electa
Page 12 Elisabetta Ferrero/Archivio White Star
Pages 14-15 Erich Lessing Archive/Contrasto
Page 17 Massimo Borchi/Archivio White Star
Page 18 left Archivio Scala
Page 18 right Bpk/Archivio Scala
Page 19 left Gianni Dagli Orti/The Art Archive
Page 19 right Massimo Borchi/Archivio White Star
Pages 20-21 Archivio Alinari, Firenze
Page 22 Massimo Borchi/Archivio White Star
Pages 22-23 Massimo Borchi/Archivio White Star
Page 23 top Massimo Borchi/Archivio White Star
Page 23 center Massimo Borchi/Archivio White Star
Page 23 bottom Massimo Borchi/Archivio White Star
Page 24 Massimo Borchi/Archivio White Star
Page 25 left Gianni Dagli Orti/The Art Archive
Page 25 right Erich Lessing Archive/Contrasto
Page 26 Massimo Borchi/Archivio White Star
Page 26 bottom Massimo Borchi/Archivio White Star
Pages 26-27 Massimo Borchi/Archivio White Star
Page 27 top Massimo Borchi/Archivio White Star
Page 27 bottom Massimo Borchi/Archivio White Star
Page 28 Gianni Dagli Orti/The Art Archive
Page 29 left Erich Lessing Archive/Contrasto
Page 29 right Gianni Dagli Orti/The Art Archive
Page 30 Justin Kerr
Pages 30-31 Justin Kerr
Pages 32-33 top Werner Forman Archive
Pages 32-33 bottom Werner Forman Archive
Page 33 left Justin Kerr
Page 33 center Justin Kerr
Page 33 right Justin Kerr
Pages 34-35 Kenneth Garrett
Page 35 Mireille Vautier/The Art Archive
Pages 36-37 Antonio Attini/Archivio White Star
Pages 38-39 Massimo Borchi/Archivio White Star
Pages 40-41 Patrick Aventurier/Gamma/Contrasto
Page 41 Massimo Borchi/Archivio White Star
Page 42 Massimo Borchi/Archivio White Star
Page 43 Massimo Borchi/Archivio White Star
Page 44 Massimo Borchi/Archivio White Star
Page 45 top Massimo Borchi/Archivio White Star
Page 45 bottom Massimo Borchi/Archivio White Star
Page 46 left Patrick Aventurier/Gamma/Contrasto
Page 46 right Aisa
Page 47 Patrick Aventurier/Gamma/Contrasto
Page 48 Patrick Aventurier/Gamma/Contrasto
Page 49 Patrick Aventurier/Gamma/Contrasto
Page 50 top Erich Lessing Archive/Contrasto
Page 50 bottom Nathan Benn/Corbis
Page 51 Gianni Dagli Orti/Corbis
Page 52 Akg-Images/Photoservice Electa
Page 53 top Akg-Images/Photoservice Electa
Page 53 bottom Werner Forman Archive
Page 54 top Akg-Images/Photoservice Electa
Page 54 bottom Akg-Images/Photoservice Electa
Page 55 Akg-Images/Photoservice Electa
Pages 56-57 Museo Archeologico Lamayeque, Sipan
Pages 58-59 Erich Lessing Archive/Contrasto
Page 59 top left Akg-Images/Photoservice Electa
Page 59 top right Heinz Plenge/Geografica EIRL
Page 59 bottom Kevin Schafer/Corbis
Page 60 top Antonio Attini/Archivio White Star
Page 60 bottom Antonio Attini/Archivio White Star
Pages 60-61 Antonio Attini/Archivio White Star
Page 61 top Antonio Attini/Archivio White Star
Page 61 bottom Antonio Attini/Archivio White Star
Page 62 top Massimo Borchi/Archivio White Star
Page 62 bottom left The British Museum
Page 62 bottom right Gianni Dagli Orti/Corbis
Page 63 Martin Beck-Coppola/Photo RMN
Page 64 top Della Zuan/Sygma/Corbis
Page 64 bottom The Bridgeman Art Library/ Archivio Alinari, Firenze
Pages 64-65 Akg-Images/Photoservice Electa
Page 66 left Dirk Antrop
Page 66 right Dirk Antrop
Pages 66-67 Dirk Antrop
Page 67 left Dirk Antrop
Page 67 right Dirk Antrop
Page 68 top Archivio Scala
Page 68 bottom left Archivio Scala
Page 68 bottom right Erich Lessing Archive/Contrasto
Page 69 Erich Lessing Archive/Contrasto
Page 70 top Antonio Attini/Archivio White Star
Page 70 bottom Bpk/Archivio Scala
Pages 70-71 Antonio Attini/Archivio White Star
Page 71 left Antonio Attini/Archivio White Star
Page 71 right Antonio Attini/Archivio White Star
Page 72 top Antonio Attini/Archivio White Star
Page 72 bottom Antonio Attini/Archivio White Star
Pages 72-73 Kenneth Garrett
Page 73 left Gianni Dagli Orti/The Art Archive
Page 73 right Antonio Attini/Archivio White Star
Page 74 Archivio White Star
Page 75 Archivio White Star
Page 76 Antonio Attini/Archivio White Star
Page 77 Archivio White Star
Page 78 Henri Stierlin

Pages 80-81 Mireille Vautier/The Art Archive
Page 81 Photoservice Electa
Page 82 Henri Stierlin
Page 83 top Photoservice Electa
Page 83 bottom left Photoservice Electa
Page 83 right Dirk Antrop
Page 84 Werner Forman Archive
Page 85 Akg-Images/Photoservice Electa
Page 86 left Justin Kerr
Page 86 center left Dirk Antrop
Page 86 center right Justin Kerr
Page 86 right Oronoz/Photo12.com
Page 87 Werner Forman Archive
Page 88 Gianni Dagli Orti/The Art Archive
Page 89 Oronoz/Photo12
Page 90 Mondadori Electa/Photoservice Electa
Page 91 Dirk Antrop
Page 92 Alison Wright/Corbis
Pages 92-93 Heinz Plenge/Geografica EIRL
Page 93 Heinz Plenge/Geografica EIRL
Page 94 left Antonio Attini/Archivio White Star
Page 94 right Antonio Attini/Archivio White Star
Page 95 Archivio White Star
Page 96 Henri Stierlin
Page 97 top Henri Stierlin
Page 97 bottom Gianni Dagli Orti/The Art Archive
Page 98 Henri Stierlin
Page 99 Henri Stierlin
Pages 100-101 Massimo Borchi/Archivio White Star
Page 101 left Dirk Antrop
Page 101 center Henri Stierlin
Page 101 right Gianni Dagli Orti/The Art Archive
Page 103 Heinz Plenge/Geografica EIRL
Page 104 Archivio White Star
Page 105 Archivio White Star
Pages 106-107 Antonio Attini/Archivio White Star
Page 107 top Antonio Attini/Archivio White Star
Page 107 center Antonio Attini/Archivio White Star
Page 107 bottom Antonio Attini/Archivio White Star
Page 108 Antonio Attini/Archivio White Star
Pages 108-109 Pablo Corral Vega/Corbis
Page 109 top Antonio Attini/Archivio White Star
Page 109 bottom Antonio Attini/Archivio White Star
Pages 110-111 Antonio Attini/Archivio White Star
Page 112 top Antonio Attini/Archivio White Star
Page 112 center Antonio Attini/Archivio White Star
Page 112 bottom Antonio Attini/Archivio White Star
Pages 112-113 Antonio Attini/Archivio White Star
Page 114 Antonio Attini/Archivio White Star
Page 115 Antonio Attini/Archivio White Star
Pages 116-117 Antonio Attini/Archivio White Star
Page 117 top Antonio Attini/Archivio White Star
Page 117 center Antonio Attini/Archivio White Star
Page 117 bottom Antonio Attini/Archivio White Star
Pages 118-119 Antonio Attini/Archivio White Star
Page 120 top Antonio Attini/Archivio White Star
Page 120 bottom Antonio Attini/Archivio White Star
Pages 120-121 Antonio Attini/Archivio White Star
Page 122 Antonio Attini/Archivio White Star
Page 123 top left Antonio Attini/Archivio White Star
Page 123 top right Antonio Attini/Archivio White Star
Page 123 bottom Antonio Attini/Archivio White Star
Page 124 Antonio Attini/Archivio White Star
Page 125 Antonio Attini/Archivio White Star
Page 126 top left Antonio Attini/Archivio White Star
Page 126 top right Antonio Attini/Archivio White Star
Page 126 bottom left e right Antonio Attini/Archivio White Star
Page 127 Antonio Attini/Archivio White Star
Pages 128-129 Antonio Attini/Archivio White Star
Page 130 Dirk Antrop
Page 131 Antonio Attini/Archivio White Star
Page 132 Massimo Borchi/Archivio White Star
Pages 132-133 Massimo Borchi/Archivio White Star
Page 133 top Massimo Borchi/Archivio White Star
Page 133 bottom Massimo Borchi/Archivio White Star
Page 134 Massimo Borchi/Archivio White Star
Pages 134-135 Charles & Josette Lenars/Corbis
Page 135 top Massimo Borchi/Archivio White Star
Page 135 bottom Massimo Borchi/Archivio White Star
Page 136 top Massimo Borchi/Archivio White Star
Page 136 center Massimo Borchi/Archivio White Star
Page 136 bottom Massimo Borchi/Archivio White Star
Pages 136-137 Massimo Borchi/Archivio White Star
Page 138 Dirk Antrop
Page 139 left Dirk Antrop
Page 139 right Dirk Antrop
Page 140 Gianni Dagli Orti/The Art Archive
Page 141 Gianni Dagli Orti/The Art Archive
Page 142 Henri Stierlin
Page 143 Henri Stierlin
Page 144 Henri Stierlin
Page 145 Gianni Dagli Orti/The Art Archive
Page 146 Jean-Gilles Berizzi/Photo RMN
Page 147 Werner Forman/Corbis
Page 148 Antonio Attini/Archivio White Star
Pages 148-149 Antonio Attini/Archivio White Star
Page 149 top Antonio Attini/Archivio White Star
Page 149 center Luciano Bitelli
Page 149 bottom Luciano Bitelli
Page 151 left Mireille Vautier/The Art Archive
Page 151 right Gianni Dagli Orti/The Art Archive
Page 152 Pablo Corral Vega/Corbis
Pages 152-153 Gary Cook/Alamy Images
Page 153 Bryan Knox/Corbis
Page 155 Dirk Antrop
Page 156 Oronoz/Photo12.com
Page 158 Bpk/Archivio Scala
Page 159 Bpk/Archivio Scala
Page 160 left Dirk Antrop
Page 160 right Dirk Antrop
Page 161 left Akg-Images/Photoservice Electa
Page 161 right top Archivio White Star
Page 161 right bottom Archivio White Star
Page 162 Archivio White Star
Page 163 top Archivio White Star
Page 163 bottom The Bridgeman Art Library/Archivio Alinari, Firenze
Page 164 Gianni Dagli Orti/The Art Archive
Page 165 left Dirk Antrop
Page 165 right Dirk Antrop
Page 166 left Archivio White Star
Page 161 right Archivio White Star
Page 167 center left Antonio Attini/Archivio White Star
Page 167 center right Bpk/Archivio Scala
Page 167 bottom Dirk Antrop
Pages 168-169 Bpk/Archivio Scala
Page 169 Bpk/Archivio Scala
Page 170 Bpk/Archivio Scala
Page 171 left Gianni Dagli Orti/The Art Archive
Page 171 right Roger Viollet/Archivio Alinari, Firenze
Page 172 Bpk/Archivio Scala
Page 173 Bpk/Archivio Scala
Page 174 Henri Stierlin
Page 175 left Henri Stierlin
Page 175 right Dirk Antrop
Pages 176-177 Dirk Antrop
Pages 178-179 Dirk Antrop
Page 180 Bowers Museum of Cultural Art/Corbis
Page 181 left Dirk Antrop
Page 181 right Dirk Antrop
Page 182 top Justin Kerr
Page 182 bottom Justin Kerr
Page 183 Dirk Antrop
Pages 184-185 Akg-Images/Photoservice Electa
Page 186 Antonio Attini/Archivio White Star
Pages 186-187 Antonio Attini/Archivio White Star
Page 187 Dirk Antrop
Page 188 Mireille Vautier/The Art Archive
Page 189 Dirk Antrop
Page 190 Bpk/Archivio Scala
Pages 190-191 Bpk/Archivio Scala
Pages 192-193 Gianni Dagli Orti/The Art Archive
Page 193 top Gianni Dagli Orti/The Art Archive
Page 193 bottom Gianni Dagli Orti/The Art Archive
Page 194 left Roger Viollet/Archivio Alinari, Firenze
Page 194 right Photo12.com
Page 195 left Photo12.com
Page 195 right Photo12.com
Page 197 left Archivio White Star
Page 197 right top Photo12.com
Page 197 right bottom Archivio Scala
Page 198 Mireille Vautier/The Art Archive
Page 199 Mireille Vautier/The Art Archive
Pages 200-201 Akg-Images/Photoservice Electa
Page 201 The Bridgeman Art Library/Archivio Alinari, Firenze
Page 202 Erich Lessing Archive/Contrasto
Page 203 Erich Lessing Archive/Contrasto
Page 208 BPK/Archivio Scala

Cover
These two golden statuettes represent Incan notables characterized by their elongated ear lobes (Museo de América, Madrid).
© *Left: Dirk Antrop - Right: Oronoz/Photo12.com*

Back cover
Left: The city of Machu Picchu was built on the orders of Inca Pachacutec in the 15th century.
© *Antonio Attini/Archivio White Star*
Right: The murals of Huaca de la Luna, one of the Moche ceremonial centers.
© *Massimo Borchi/Archivio White Star*

Abbreviations used in the captions
MAAHUN: Museo de Arqueología Antropología e Historia de la Universidad Nacional, Trujillo

208 - THIS EMBOSSED GOLD PLATE REPRESENTS A MONSTROUS BEING WITH EXTREMITIES IN THE SHAPE OF SNAKE/FELINE. IT WAS FOUND IN THE PACHACAMAC CEREMONIAL CENTER. THE CENTER FELL UNDER HUARI INFLUENCE DURING THE MIDDLE HORIZON (ETHNOLOGISCHES MUSEUM, BERLIN).